P

QUE

RECLAIM YOUR CROWN WHEN LIFE
KNOCKS YOU DOWN

"*Queen Up!* takes a fascinating new approach to the ancient art of Tarot. By focusing in great depth on just four cards—the Queens in the different suits—Angela Kaufman shows us how we can use the cards not just to understand our lives, but to transform them."

—**Rachel Pollack**, author of
The Fissure King: A Novel in Five Stories

"Angela Kaufman has created an impactful book that draws you in with each page you read. It is, indeed, empowering and relevant to women of all ages. Read it, and you will find yourself in it."

—**Tina M. Zion**, bestselling author of
Become a Medical Intuitive and *Advanced Medical Intuition*

"Take Jung's archetypes, mix in Tarot, add guidance from someone knowledgeable in the ways of psychology and magic, and you have *Queen Up!*—an insanely accessible guide to becoming a more complete person."

—**Rebecca Elson**, publisher of *The Magical Buffet* website

"*Queen Up* is a delightful exploration of the self using timeless methods. Kaufman has beautifully given readers a tool for increasing their confidence and reaching their goals that is both spiritual and practical. When reading this book, I feel like I'm in a helpful, insightful, and fun coaching session with Kaufman. A great read!"

—**Courtney Weber**, author of
Tarot for One: The Art of Reading for Yourself

"With *Queen Up!* Angela Kaufman has given us a jolt of inspiration to reclaim our inborn sovereignty and magic. This is important, rewarding work at a crucial juncture in history, and my deep wish is that every feminine person alive step into her queenhood. *Queen Up!* offers thoughtful and practical guidance to start you on this fulfilling path of ruling the elements of your world rather than being ruled. So take the journey Kaufman offers here, and expand your royalty."

—**Carolyn Elliott**, PhD, founder of *WITCH* magazine (*badwitch.es*) and author of *Existential Kink* and *Awaken Your Genius*

"*Queen Up!* is an abundance of inspiration! Angela Kaufman's extraordinary book offers numerous means to activate our Goddess-given power. With *Queen Up!* we delve into powerful archetypes and learn to incorporate them into our daily lives. We learn rituals to access our intuitive knowledge and are offered practical tips to help align with these powerful archetypes. Throughout *Queen Up!* are exercises that guide us toward a deeper sense of self. *Queen Up!* has it all. The times they are a-changing. We women are finding our voice, our power, our creative force. *Queen Up!* is a tool to help us women achieve our greatest potential."

—**Lisa Levart**, photographer and author of *Goddess on Earth: Portraits of the Divine Feminine*

QUEEN UP!

RECLAIM YOUR CROWN WHEN
LIFE KNOCKS YOU DOWN

QUEEN UP!

RECLAIM YOUR CROWN WHEN LIFE KNOCKS YOU DOWN

*Unleash the Power of
Your Inner Tarot Queen*

ANGELA KAUFMAN

FOREWORD BY HEATHERASH AMARA

Conari Press

This edition first published in 2018 by Conari Press,
an imprint of
Red Wheel/Weiser, LLC
With offices at:
65 Parker Street, Suite 7
Newburyport, MA 01950
www.redwheelweiser.com

ISBN: 978-1-57324-732-0
Library of Congress Cataloging-in-Publication Data available upon request.

Cover design by Jim Warner
Cover artwork by Shaheen Miro
Typeset in Sabon

Printed in Canada
MAR
10 9   8 7 6   5 4 3 2 1

This book is dedicated to Patricia Gardner, Dayna Winters,
and to all women who find themselves at the crossroads.

CONTENTS

PART THREE:
52 WEEKS TO QUEEN UP
Your Year of Empowered Living

APPENDIX

FOREWORD

Words can point our mind in the direction of transformation, but symbols and archetypes speak directly to our psyche to unlock our inner wisdom and intuition. In a world where we are inundated with words and concepts, it is vital for us to reach back into the past and ask for guidance and support from the wisdom of our ancestors who knew the power of images and energy.

Women today are often woefully lacking in solid, feminine role models, or, if we do have someone who inspires us, we can compromise the healing available through the connection with our own judgment and comparison.

Many years ago I discovered the power of archetypes while studying with my first teacher, Vicki Noble, cocreator of *The Motherpeace Tarot*. At first, I didn't understand the importance of these archetypical images or how vital they would become in my life. How could a bunch of pictures help me to know myself better, reclaim my power, and find my voice? But as I started working with the cards by sitting with one image of the major arcana a day, I soon discovered which of the different archetypical expressions felt like home and which ones felt foreign or uncomfortable. And that willingness to listen to the different resonances or discordant notes of each image led to a deepening intimacy with myself and a pathway to shed comparison and claim what my energy aligned with.

Today, when I get stuck in my life I always turn to some form of divination to remind me of what quality I am missing or need to adjust in my life. I find the symbols bypass any "should" or "must" that my mind can sometimes get stuck on, and take me straight into the heart of what my soul has to remind me.

While each of us is a unique expression of life, we each resonate with four main frequencies of archetypical energy that are aligned with the four elements: air, fire, water, and earth. While we each hold all four of these energies within us, we often align with one main element. Knowing the element we are kin with and the qualities and gifts of that element help us to know ourselves and our expression, and can help us take action in a way that supports rather than hinders us.

As the mama of the Warrior Goddess movement, an archetype of the divine feminine that I believe is much needed today, I'm passionate about helping women find their inner strength. This is why I so appreciate Angela's *Queen Up!* and her powerful re-visioning of the Tsarot's queen of wands, swords, cups, and pentacles as a way to guide women to harness and express their inner potential. Just as we need more warrior goddess women, we need more women who have claimed their archetypical queen: their sovereignty, wisdom, and strength.

As Angela explains, these energies are not outside of ourselves, though it can be immensely helpful to imagine the four queens as motivating, comforting, inspiring forces that are watching out for us. The real gifts come when we embody the energy of all four qualities and discover our innate creativity, courage, love, and patience.

Whether you choose to simply focus on one of the queen archetypes to guide you, or you go deeply into the 52-week, year long empowerment process in part three, may the words and beautiful images in this book bring you into right relationship with yourself and help you to "queen up" and reclaim your crown with grace, even during difficult times.

—HeatherAsh Amara,
author of the bestselling *Warrior Goddess Training*

INTRODUCTION

L ike most women, I began adulthood with a plan. After six years of college and with a new career in social work, I was eager to serve others as a professional while cultivating my intuitive, spiritual connection as a personal calling. Also like most women, I was forced to contend with an unexpected twist of fate. Yes, even psychics have surprises!

I was struck by a car as a pedestrian in 2009. Multiple broken bones and a lacerated lung healed within months, but a mild traumatic brain injury remained. My priority, at the time, had been to get back to life as I knew it. I faced obstacles, especially in my career. To heal, I needed to let go of my plans and the self-image to which I was attached.

Before the accident, I was the "smart one" and had no problem embracing the labels, titles, and boxes that go along with being an academic overachiever. Now, my memory and energy level were impaired, resulting in challenges I was not used to. Even with the support of family, friends, and treatment, healing was a slow, difficult process.

Spiritual exploration, previously a significant aspect of my lifestyle, now became essential to my healing journey. Beliefs such as "everything is energy" and the practice of "aligning with natural elements" took on a new purpose. Starting a new life and healing from my injury were not intellectual exercises but an energetic process. I had to slow my pace, meditate more, and rest—all factors that also foster greater connection with Spirit and intuition.

Previously an avid reader, I now struggled to retain information from books, and reading gave me migraines. In my old life, I easily expended energy, but now felt constantly fatigued. Adapting to a lifestyle of rest and a hiatus from books felt like sitting in a perpetual time-out chair while the rest of the world was free to play.

One day during a meditation, my guides made it clear that I did not need to view my limitations as punishment, but as an opportunity to break through the true limitations of placing value only on certain abilities while ignoring others. The ability to gather information from books and classes was of no higher value than the ability to perceive and receive information from Spirit and intuition during periods of rest. I came to understand that I still had access to vast resources. My life was only devastated to the extent that I was clinging to remnants of an old identity that no longer fit the emerging circumstances. Rather than lamenting the person I used to be, I could tap into the various archetypes within and find healing, integration, and most importantly, a future.

As a student of both psychology and spirituality, I understood that people have access to various archetypal selves. We all outwardly align with one dominant aspect of personality, but inherently we carry the energy of numerous other aspects of Self. For example, someone who is courageous (Warrior archetype energy) can find it within herself to also be calm and nurturing (Mother archetype energy). These latent energies can be brought out either by circumstance or conscious intention. This understanding provided a holistic perspective on the energies of empowerment and personality.

Drawing on these principles, I sought to realign my energy and sense of purpose by harmonizing the aspects of myself not given their due credit prior to the brain injury. Through this process, I realized how many women were also facing significant transitions—perhaps not brain injury, but ones that were shaking the core of their foundation as individuals. After divorces, losses of career, health crises— they were left asking, "Who am I? Where am I going? What do I *do* now?" What if all women could understand how much power exists in aspects of themselves not yet realized? What if they could break out of their boxes, their titles, their labels?

The Queen Up system blends various metaphysical teachings and psychological concepts, which will empower you to navigate life's most challenging situations. In part one, we will explore the basic tenets that inform this system. In part two, we will meet the four Tarot Queens who embody this process and learn how to access their energies as well as look at common obstacles. Finally, in part three, we will take on a week-by-week journey to a more empowered way of living.

Part One

WHO IS YOUR
INNER QUEEN?

What if you had the power to awaken your full potential? Would you be willing to honor your dreams at any price? Even if it causes you doubts, fears, and costs you the comfort of what you find familiar? Are you ready to Queen Up?

Every woman has the capacity to rise to personal power in any situation by connecting to the four archetypal sources of energy within. You may already be acquainted with one of these sources: this is the talent or special gift most natural to you.

To Queen Up when life gets messy, you must align with your highest wisdom, your integrated self.

The system outlined in this book is intended to create a working relationship with the archetypal energies within and connect to your Higher Self. The essential archetypes are the Four Queens as represented in the Tarot; they are representations of four different key forces necessary for balance. Each Queen symbolizes a quintessential part of our personality as well as our experience of being human. We all possess each of the energies embodied by the Four Queens, who are not beings outside of ourselves, but a part of who we are. In the Queen Up system, we will imagine the Four Queens as external figures only for the sake of simplicity—in order to visualize a motivating, comforting, inspiring force. As such it is important to distinguish that while the Queen card from any Tarot deck (and even some substitute cards from more unique decks) can be used to anchor you on your journey, the cards themselves are accessories. The power lies within you.

Whether you use your favorite Tarot deck or just a regular deck of playing cards, or even create your own Inner Queen cards, this system is flexible and not limited to just one corresponding deck.

The Queens represent four aspects of feminine power. Once a woman knows how to access these four sources of power, she has the potential to become an intuitive, creative, unstoppable force. This book will take you on that journey of discovery and empowerment. On this path, you will find your power of inspiration (Queen of Wands), passion (Queen of Swords), love (Queen of Cups), and abundance (Queen of Pentacles). Working with the four Tarot Queens makes it easier to validate an abstract concept because we are putting a "face" on it—as we tend to do with spirits, angels, gods and goddesses, and so forth. It is also easier for many women to imagine a persona representing who they aspire to be than it is for them to see themselves in that energy.

The Queens serve as a symbol of the potential of every woman.

ENERGY IS EVERYTHING

Ancient people believed in the power of energy and sought connection with this force as Spirit or ether through ritual, art, chanting, singing, drumming, and other practices. Our understanding of and relationship to energy has been repackaged over the centuries. We access energy in the form of electricity to provide modern conveniences, for example. Yet we are also rediscovering the concept of energy as personal power. Quantum physics tests the limits of what we believe about physical reality, and we recognize that flowing, changing currents of energy are at the root of all life and are shaped by both thought and observation.

Scientist and inventor Nikola Tesla said, "If you want to find the secrets of the universe, think in terms of energy, frequency, and vibration." All things are energy vibrating at different frequencies. We lose sight of this when we are taught to perceive through only our five physical senses. A table appears to be a physical structure: a plank held up by four legs. But if we remember the role of energy and vibration, we understand a table is energy that vibrates at the frequency of physical matter with physical attributes commonly recognized and described as being a "table."

Relationships, emotions, states of mind, and even the events occurring in our lives can be understood on a deeper level if we remember they are currents of energy vibrating in ways that attract or repel other forms of energy. All beings are made up of energy. It is a matter of simplicity to perceive physical objects as somehow more real than abstract things like thought or emotion. There is no separation. All life is an endless energy tapestry. Energy vibrates at different levels. The feeling of these different "vibes" is often used to describe anything from auras to intuition to the vibe of a room. It is all energy: one big buffet, but with different flavors.

To sample the best of the variety of life's flavors, we can align ourselves with different types of energies. We do this in a variety of ways. The main vehicle for energy movement is thought. Even as you read this book—which is energy vibrating at the level of paper and ink— you are attuning to the vibration created by the concepts spelled out by these letters. In other words, your mind is opening to new thoughts or remembering concepts you may already know.

You may be comfortable with these notions, or they may unsettle you. Either way, your energy is attuning to the concept described in these paragraphs. Without being conscious of it, you are aligning your energy with the focus of becoming empowered. That is, after all, the reason you began reading this book, isn't it?

Thought is a simple mechanism for focusing energy, but it is not the only vehicle, nor is it always the most efficient. For example, you may have numerous thoughts that contradict each other, some thoughts with high emotional attachment to them, and other thoughts with minimal emotional backing. Thus, energy can be dissipated. In pop culture terms "working the law of attraction" is associated with power of thought but may not take these other factors into consideration. Thoughts can backfire, aligning you with what you don't want. Take for example the case of someone who is preoccupied with her own shortcomings. Each anxiety-laden worry aligns such a person with the outcome she dreads, and periodically the self-sabotage of planting the seeds of anxiety come to fruition in situations this person hoped to avoid.

Spiritual Mechanics

The four Tarot Queens in the Queen Up system are representations of four key sources of energy necessary for wholeness and balance. Keeping energy in alignment fosters intuitive growth and confidence. As a more empowered woman, your energy will help attract the types of relationships you desire. Your energy will also attract opportunities of all kinds, because you will be working from your highest expression of Self and attuning to your purpose and passion, rather than aligning with your fears and limitations.

You do not need to be a "spiritual mechanic" to keep your energy in alignment. Yet like your car, your body—as the vehicle carrying your spirit or energy—is subject to the wear and tear of everyday life. Like your car, your personal energy faces bumps in the road, suffers the damage of corrosive environmental elements, and will naturally fall out of alignment.

What types of "potholes" impact your spirit? There are disappointments, criticism, fear, doubts, unmet expectations, trauma, grief, and various other aspects of life.

Shamans practice soul retrieval based on the belief that major losses cause the soul to fragment, resulting in emotional wounds. Psychologists who study trauma are familiar with the ways in which survivors lose a part of themselves in the past. Healing demands the reintegration of all the aspects of one's soul.

You needn't suffer a significant trauma to lose the balance and alignment of your personal energy. Everyday disappointments and challenges can pull your personal energy in various directions. We work too hard, succumbing to our personal obsessions and addictions. We overvalue some aspects of ourselves, and undervalue others. In some cases, women have been taught to undervalue all aspects of themselves!

Just like a car may need realignment even when driven by the most cautious driver, so too do our own energies need balancing, even when we are surrounded by the most loving people with the best intentions. Thought, intention, meditation, creative expression, movement, and visualization are all practices that keep energy in alignment. On the path to empowerment outlined in this book, you will practice various techniques to align your energy.

We do not have overt control over events in our lives or over people we know, but we do have control over the energy we exude and what it draws to or repels from us. We call this awareness of energy *consciousness*. In the mid-twentieth century, Maharishi Mahesh Yogi proposed that concentrated efforts of only 1 percent of the population practicing a specific meditation technique would alter the energy of group consciousness enough to reduce crime rates. His theory, known as the Maharishi Effect, has been tested successfully in dozens of scientifically controlled studies around the world in communities impacted by crime. How is this possible? It works because energy is changeable and alignment of thought (intent) and consistent practice of this alignment produces tangible results. Modern popular culture calls this the Law of Attraction, the belief that by focusing on positive or negative thoughts, people invite positive or negative experiences into their life. The concept also finds a voice in the expression, "What you sow you shall reap."

There is nothing new about this phenomenon; it has been described for centuries in various cultures and belief systems around the world. While many will apply the Law of Attraction to manifest changes in their lives, or employ the Maharishi Effect to promote social change, few are exploring ways in which the individual can apply the laws of energy to invite profound personal change. In this book, we will explore in greater detail working with energy and the profound effects it will have on your life.

From "Woo-Woo" to "Guru"

The energetic nature of all things, a concept once considered "out there" but now commonly scientifically accepted, is also a premise for the Queen Up system. If all things are energy and energy is change-able and influenced by the expectations of the observer, then we can actively participate in the cocreation of our lives.

It is no longer frowned upon to be conscious of greater potential for growth and transcendence. We are embracing, rather than shun-ning, those who would see the value of personal evolution through spiritual mechanics. In fact, we seek instruction from modern gurus, but this system introduces readers to the divine feminine gurus within—the Queens.

Mystical Wisdom for Modern Women

In addition to understanding the power and pervasiveness of energy, we need to look at some mystical practices to set the stage for the Queen Up system. The following eclectic metaphysical and spiritual concepts are essential to getting to the heart of the Queen Up system, and most important among them is the concept of working with archetypes.

While some of the core components of the Queen Up system may seem strange to modern women in western society, the underlying philosophy is really not new or uncommon. Cultures around the world believe in the connection between energy, personality, wellness, and reality. To help bridge the gap between mystical and modern thought we will take a tour of several examples of energy cosmology and their relationship to the Queen Up system. Consider this section your initiation into the realm of intuitive thought as opposed to conventional western logical thought. The Queen Up system will help you connect to your intuition by bringing your awareness beyond the conscious thoughts of the logical, rational mind and into your own intuitive center.

Archetypes

An archetype is a symbol so pervasive and widely recognized that it spans time and culture. When you get to know the individual Queen archetypes, you'll get a better handle on what that entails. Various systems are based on archetypes, such as Tarot and astrology. In fact, many people who have taken the journey to connect to their Inner Queen remark that it is similar to having their astrological chart read. The information gleaned will reflect the same elemental archetypes visible to an astrologer reading a natal chart. However, the Queen Up system is also intended to give access to all the archetypes via *intention*. One need not succumb to only following the drives of a guiding sign or planet, but can instead harness those drives or shift energy to align with the strengths of any of the planetary archetypes.

Those familiar with the concepts of elemental energies will recognize the archetypes of the Queens as personifications of the four elements of Air, Fire, Water, and Earth.

The archetypal language of Queening Up draws on the Tarot, and those who have studied Tarot will recognize the archetypes as embodied in the Tarot Queens. As stated in detail throughout this book, the Queens represent four distinct energies, personality types, and life areas based on an understanding of archetypes. The connection between image, symbol, archetype, and individual intuition can be personal.

Metaphysical practitioners have developed several ways of working with the Tarot archetypes, depending on background and training. Those who follow traditional interpretations read Wands as related to the element of Fire, thus corresponding to the Queen of Swords in the Queen Up system. Likewise, Swords are read as the element of Air, or corresponding in this system to the Queen of Wands. The Air/Fire suit correspondences do vary from deck to deck. Many like myself, whose reading style reflects the cosmology of the pagan/Wiccan tradition, read Wands as Air and Swords as Fire.

In the Queen Up system, the Inner Queen of Wands corresponds to the element of Air and the powers of the mind. What do you associate with the Air? Leaves? Wind? Fans? What do you associate with the mind? Computers? Language? Numbers?

The Inner Queen of Swords corresponds to Fire and the powers of will, motivation, and justice. She is the Warrior Queen. What do you associate with fire and warrior energy? Spears? Torches? Armor?

The Inner Queen of Cups is associated with Water and nurturing, emotions, and maternal energy as well as love. Symbolically her energy can be represented by many things such as hearts or seashells or mirrors.

As ruler of the Earth element and the realm of abundance, the Inner Queen of Pentacles is associated with physical health, wealth, work, and comfort. What images or symbols do you associate with this energy? Dollar signs? Gold coins? Jewels? Stones?

Understanding these connections will help you interpret the symbolism in any deck you choose to work with. For example, if you have a Tarot deck that contains a Queen of Feathers, you may associate feathers not only with birds, flight, and the sky but also with early writing instruments like quill pens. Therefore you may use this Queen to represent the Queen of Wands in the Queen Up system. Likewise a deck containing a Queen of Seashells may make you think of the ocean, the water element, and emotions, love, etc. Thus she would correspond to the Queen of Cups in the Queen Up system.

In the appendix of this book you will find a listing of several different Tarot decks, and how they correspond to the Queen Up system.

Synchronicity

There are no coincidences, no accidents, and any information we seek can be gained through the power of intention and an open mind. This concept of right timing was promoted by psychologist Carl Jung.

It is no coincidence you are reading these words right now: Ask a question, and a solution will be given. And when the Queen cards are shuffled and an intention is set, and when a card is drawn, there is nothing random about the information received.

The Queen Up system requires a mind open to receiving information through this belief in divine timing.

It's All About Balance

Ayurveda, TCM, Humorism, and Energy Cosmology

The Indian practice of Ayurveda teaches that all of creation—whether human, nonhuman animals, or other aspects of the natural world—is composed of fundamental energy elements called *doshas*. According to Ayurveda, all beings must maintain a balance of these fundamental characteristics. In Ayurveda, mindfulness of the balance between the doshic energies is essential to living a healthy, harmonious life. In this system, everything from season to diet to environmental factors can work to heal, accentuate, or aggravate an individual's doshic makeup. It is important not to create an imbalance in the doshas through poor diet or lifestyle habits, and a greater understanding of personality and relationships can be found by examining the order of greatest to least dominance of doshic energy. The doshas describe not only our personalities but also the constitution of our physical body.

Similar beliefs around the elemental forces of the natural world and within the personality and physical structure of all living beings are the basis for traditional Chinese medicine (TCM). If you have ever tried tai chi or qigong or had an acupuncture or shiatsu treatment, then you are experiencing a healing and rebalancing of the energy in your mind, body, and spirit through a very technical process that is at once a science, a cosmology, and an art form in its own right. TCM is based on a system of five elements corresponding to the fundamental energies of the natural world. Like Ayurveda, TCM teaches that the optimal health and functioning of an individual on every level require harmonizing and balancing of these fundamental energies within oneself and in one's surroundings. Just as certain dietary or environmental conditions would aggravate the doshas in the Ayurvedic worldview, so too would one seek dietary or environmental conditions to accentuate specific elemental energies, while avoiding foods or situations that would trigger imbalance or disharmony, among the five elements of TCM. Even western medicine has its ancient roots in this elemental cosmology.

The concept of Humorism holds that there are four temperaments known as humors. Hippocrates drew on this system for much of his work in diagnosing or treating illness. Distress was seen as a result of imbalanced humors within the body, and this was also linked to personality energy. The four humors were connected to one's behavior, personality, emotional state, and physical being. Students of astrology also connected the four humors with the four elements and thus grouped the zodiac signs by temperament (melancholic, sanguine, phlegmatic, choleric). While this concept would seem strange to current allopathic western medicine practitioners, humorism has evolved and is more easily recognized in the realm of psychological personality typing. The Myers–Briggs Personality Inventory, for example, draws on the concept of dominant personality styles and tendencies, while losing the emphasis on elemental energies.

Ayurveda, Humorism, and TCM are fascinating systems that are far more intricate than this book can explore; however, the primary concept worth noting is the cosmology and beliefs uniting these systems. They all stem from cultural/spiritual beliefs in the interconnectedness of all things. This may seem foreign at first to those of us living in modern western cultures, where we are taught that people are substantially and essentially different from nature and that food, environment, personality, the physical body, the mind, the spirit, and life events are all distinct, unique, and separate. Even modern belief in the mind-body connection tends to halt at a surface level of understanding. We aren't given the tools and resources to go deeper into this awareness that mind, body, spirit, and nature are all a web of connections and inform each other, to say nothing of the implications for what this truly means. Thus, some of the concepts in this book may seem familiar, yet also challenge conventional belief. It is best to integrate these concepts with our modern understanding of science, medicine, and the like, rather than seeing them as competing worldviews.

The core concept behind Ayurveda, TCM, humorism, and the Queen Up systems, as well as some others we will explore, is the idea that natural elements are a part of our fundamental constitution as individuals. Just as one may be described as having a "fiery" nature, we recognize that the energetic force that gives fire the ability to warm or consume also operates within our bodies and psyches, giving the individual the ability to be energized or obsessive, for example. From this standpoint we can begin to really grasp what it means to be beings of energy connected to a world also created from the same elemental energies. We can also begin to understand what it means to be able to access the energies within, draw on and balance them, and heal ourselves and our lives through their power.

Like Ayurveda, Humorism, and TCM, the Queen Up system recognizes that each person embodies the energies of all the archetypal Queens and thus is not destined to operate on a default basis, fueled by the specific set of drives of one Queen only. This system embraces the humanist standpoint that we may evolve in consciousness and align with different energy to attain new—and hopefully, more desirable—results in life.

The Queen Up system is designed to help women accentuate and shift from one source of energy to another, similar to the aforementioned systems. Also in this way, the Tarot path to empowerment bears similarities to alchemy. That discipline's refining and purifying energy in the desire to turn "lead into gold" is thought to be symbolic of the purification of the spirit.

Put simply, thoughts become things. Thus, we can shift our experience of reality, including who we perceive ourselves to be, by shifting our intention and aligning with different energy.

Spirit Guides

Various spiritual paths honor Spirit Guides even if specific cultural or spiritual traditions may vary on what constitutes a Spirit Guide: family or loved ones who have passed on, angels, or other beings who work with us as guides, teachers, and protectors. We all have guides and have experienced their presence in our lives, whether we have been consciously aware of it or not. The subtle recognition of a warning to take a detour, only to later learn that in doing so you avoided an accident, or the subdued nudging to apply for a job you would have overlooked only to ace the interview and get hired, would be examples of ways our guides influence our intuition to help us on our journey.

Many excellent books exist with the sole focus of connecting readers to their guides. For the purposes of the Queen Up system, it is helpful to be open to the idea that we have access to the wisdom, love, healing, and guidance of benevolent energies who are always with us. A common misconception is that Spirit Guides must appear visually, identify themselves by name, and begin listing instructions on what to do. Spirit Guides are manifestations of subtle energy and will connect best when invited to do so. Commonly you will perceive images, symbols, scenes, colors, words, sounds, smells, or sensations as your guide's way of giving you a message. Note that guides can use any of your senses to convey information, not just sight. Also, information is typically symbolic. For example, if a guide wants to share that a new opportunity is on the horizon, the guide may show you an image of a sunrise. Guides will work through the senses and through symbols and archetypes that resonate with you. It is by interpreting these symbols and archetypes that the message is understood.

The Queen Up system operates from an intuitive mind-set through which you will be able to effectively and easily receive insights from your guides. For many of the exercises in this book, your guides will be described as the Four Queens. Remember that the Queens represent archetypal energies that your guides will align with to convey their messages to you.

If your spiritual beliefs do not encompass work with Spirit Guides that is okay. Simply consider the guidance as coming from your Higher Self, Higher Wisdom, or an aspect of yourself that transcends the ego and is connected to your larger purpose and path. Throughout this book, the terms Higher Self and Spirit Guides are often used interchangeably to embrace a variety of spiritual and personal beliefs.

As you embark on your mystical path to empowerment, you are not only finding empowerment for yourself, you are also strengthening your intuition and connection to your Higher Self and Spirit Guides.

Thought Forms

If everything is energy and energy is fueled by words, thoughts, beliefs, attitudes, emotions, and actions, then thought forms can be described as beliefs, thoughts, or even emotional experiences that have been given so much energy that they become palpable in your consciousness. Have you ever been so engrossed in a book or movie that you began to feel like the characters had become a part of your life? Have you ever heard the words of a parent or influential figure in your mind and felt as if you were carrying that person around with you, even though they were far away or even deceased?

Thought forms are constructs, abstract concepts that represent beliefs and emotional states. They can be created intentionally or unintentionally and are neither bad nor good, but the energy we give to them can influence how we feel about ourselves and our lives. For example, a woman who works with a hypnotherapist to create a visual symbol to remind her that she is strong, healthy, and secure without cigarettes is using the power of a thought form to kick the habit of smoking. When this person is reminded of this symbol, she is consciously strengthening her own energy as a nonsmoker through the use of this thought form. A child who is afraid to go to sleep because he believes a monster lives under his bed is unknowingly investing his energy in a belief in a scary monster. Thus the child may interpret shadows or other stimuli as being the work of this monster. When we consistently sabotage certain areas of our life or feel restricted or blocked by old beliefs or fears, we are giving energy to thought forms, and when we embark on a journey of transformation, thought forms can work to our benefit. A woman who begins a diet with an image of herself healthy and strong is creating this thought form as a means to remain motivated.

This work will show you how to recognize the self-defeating thought forms you may be carrying from past experiences or fears of potential experiences that have not occurred. Once you are able to recognize these thought forms and the ways in which you energetically feed into them, you are then free to release this energy and intentionally create empowering, positive beliefs that carry the same strength. Rather than carrying energetic souvenirs of what you don't want in your life, you are free to create tokens and symbols of what you are striving for.

Psychology, Personality & the Queens

Psychologists described the Self as comprised of various drives including the ego and internal conflicting drives such as the Shadow (the aspect of the Self perceived as wild or dangerous). When the ego, Shadow, and other aspects of personality are kept in balance, the individual is stable and adapts to life with greater ease. When an aspect of personality is suppressed, imbalance and disturbance ensue. This system is aligned with methods of personal development that attempt to balance the internal and external, acceptable and feared aspects of the Self.

Studies demonstrate a connection between mind-set, energy, attitude, and feelings. In addition, well-being, health, and recovery are also implicated as results of energy and intention. Studies on the efficacy of meditation, group consciousness, and the like are giving credibility to the power of intention to create reality. The consistent thread is energy. It is the pattern of energy that is intentionally being accessed and altered to generate healing and integration.

Finally, my own experience as both a licensed clinical social worker and practicing certified intuitive consultant and intuitive relationship coach have allowed me to show people tools that help them become conscious of and change their energy. The women I have had the privilege of coaching experience personal transformation, including improved relationships, because of meeting their Inner Queen and discovering tools for continuing their own intuitive connection to the power of energy.

As you continue to explore this path, you may begin to connect intuitively to various energies in nature, other people, animals, and circumstances. You are awakening to senses long dormant. Enjoy this process of connecting to the divine power within!

LEGEND OF THE FOUR QUEENS

Once upon a time, there lived four sisters. To the world, they seemed unexceptional, average, everyday women.

These were no ordinary women, however, for they knew an ancient truth:

All attitudes, beliefs, and thoughts carry energy, and energy can be converted to physical matter. They discovered each had special powers . . . powers of the mind, heart, will, and physical strength.

Together they overcame odds manifesting love, health, and wealth and welcoming unexpected success.

Then a strange thing happened.

As each came to depend on the power of her sisters, strength gave way to weakness. Each began to deny her inner light, seeking only the strength of the others. Relying only on the strength of their sisters, their inner light began to fade . . . until they learned their greatest lesson: Although their sisterhood was a blessing, the power each sought from the others could also be found within.

Thus, they discovered true alchemy: By harnessing the four powers of the soul each was transformed from woman to Queen.

Their power was incomplete without an understanding of the Four Divine Decrees:

♛ All things are energy—even thoughts, beliefs, and attitudes—and energy becomes matter.

♛ Energy is changeable.

♛ Energy contains elements of its opposite.

♛ Energy can be accessed at will through the power of intention; thus anything required to succeed can be found within.

Every woman is the Queen of her own destiny. The power of girl-friends can help you discover your inner strengths, but the ability to harness and balance the many powers within makes one a Queen.

Prepare to embark on your own mystical path to empowerment by discovering your true power.

Part Two

YOUR JOURNEY
BEGINS

Follow this guide with an open mind and open heart. Invite your creativity and write, sketch, or doodle the insights and intuitive answers that come as you explore your inner power. Every woman is unique, and your path to meet your Inner Queen will reflect this.

You are about to be introduced to each of the archetypal Queens. In order of appearance in this work, they are the Queen of Wands, Queen of Swords, Queen of Cups, and Queen of Pentacles. The following sections will give you an up close and personal look at each specific Queen.

As you complete the workbook-type exercises, you will have the opportunity to get to know the energy of the Four Queens as if they are people you would encounter in daily life. Remember their energies are found in the personalities of those you encounter, but most importantly, their energies are a part of who *you* are.

Suggested Guide to Meeting Your Inner Queen

The Chronological Path

To use the workbook exercises chronologically, start at the beginning and complete the reflective exercises in order.

You can also use the cards as daily reminders and meditation tools to help connect to the Queens on a deeper level. You will learn specific techniques to work with the cards in these ways later in the book.

The Intuitive Path

You may also choose to use the Queen Up system according to your intuition and inner guidance. To do this, take a moment and look at the images of each Queen in the beginning of her chapter. Try not to think about the meaning or what you are "supposed to" do. Rather, allow yourself to be in an open and receptive state. Where do you feel pulled to begin? Are you captivated by the energy you feel from the Queen of Cups? If so, start with her, even though her chapter is not first. Do you feel intrigued by the Queen of Swords? Great! Trust your intuition has guided you to focus on her for a reason. You may also center yourself and ask whose energy you most need to get acquainted with at this time.

Instructions for the Intuitive Path with Cards

Review the Common Tarot Decks and Queen Up Correspondences in the appendix of this book. As this system is universal, you may use the four Inner Queen cards printed on the cover flaps of this book (and available for order at *intuitiveangela.com*) or you may use the Queen cards from your preferred Tarot deck or even from a standard set of playing cards. Choose whichever queen image speaks to you most directly. Once you have selected your Queen cards, proceed to the following exercise.

Quiet your mind and set the intention that you will find the Queen with whom you most strongly relate now, at this point in your life.

Shuffle the cards and, without looking, randomly place all four in a row in front of you.

- ♛ The first card will show you which Queen to begin with and represents your dominant energy now.

- ♛ The second represents your next most comfortable energy.

- ♛ The third represents your Shadow Queen, whose energy poses a significant challenge to you at this time.

- ♛ The fourth represents the energy you seem to have lost.

Using this template as a guide, you may choose to start with your comfort zone or with your least comfortable energy or skip around between the various Queens. You may also decide to choose a card each time you use this journal and continually work on that Queen in accordance with the result of each individual card drawn.

You cannot do it wrong. Your intuition is guiding you; let it loose, and go with it!

As an example of the Intuitive Path with cards, if shuffling reveals first the Queen of Cups, then Swords, then Pentacles, and finally Wands, then go to the section in part two of this book that focuses on the Queen of Cups. Complete the exercises associated with this Queen so that you can develop a deep connection with her energy and lessons, and then move on to the exercises for each following Queen.

As you seek guidance for different aspects of your life, repeat this process and revisit the lessons from your Queens. If all things are energy and energy is changeable, then it is necessary to bring energy into alignment for the benefit of your growth and well-being periodically.

Whether you complete this journal in order or explore the various Queens based on your intuition, you will find the process empowering and transformative. Follow your heart and enjoy the journey! Part two of this book provides practical tips for aligning with the energy of the Queens and building the bridge to trusting your intuition and higher guidance. The next section, 52 Weeks to Queen Up, provides a year's worth of exercises to help you use this system to manifest your desires and harmonize the energies in your life by focusing on weekly activities to strengthen your journey through the year. The final part of this book contains an Intuitive Log to help you get comfortable trusting your inner compass.

You may use the Inner Queen Intuitive Log in tandem with the 52 Weeks to Queen Up section or work on each separately. You may also choose to revisit any of the exercises at any time. Each experience strengthens your journey and brings you deeper into connection with the Queen within.

QUEEN OF WANDS

Ruler of the Mind and Creativity

The Wise Mentor

Creativity • Communication • Imagination • Adaptability

Meeting the Queen of Wands

The Queen of Wands rules the territory of the mind. In some Tarot traditions, the suit of Wands is associated with the element of Fire (or the description of the Queen of Swords in this system), but for our purposes she aligns with the element of Air. She also may be called by different names such as the Queen of Rods, Queen of Clubs, Queen of Air, etc. For your convenience, the appendix identifies this Queen from various decks.

When you experience brilliance, insight, and creativity, you are drawing on the power of the Queen of Wands. The power of thought and the spoken word are the domain of this Queen. She offers the strength to take an idea and weave it into manifestation or open the mind to embracing the potential that exists in fantasy and then sculpting this potential into reality. When you ponder philosophical questions or daydream, or "think outside the box" and change your perspective, you are harnessing the energy of the Queen of Wands.

Think of the word *imagination*. The act of thinking has just connected you to the Queen of Wands. Imagination starts with an "image," and when the image in your mind is transformed into a concrete reality, you have used the power of the Queen of Wands to manifest something through the channel of your mind's creativity. This is the seed of all things. Everything that exists in the physical world began in the creative energy of the Mind.

The Queen of Wands also rules communication, because we take what starts in the mind and express it through words, writing, art, music, dance, body language, and other forms of connection.

The power of the Queen of Wands gives you the ability to generate new ideas, plans, and visions for yourself and your life. It is the power to access imagination and ask yourself, "What else could be possible if I were not attached to what I believe must be possible?"

In that regard, the Queen of Wands embodies the power of belief, for belief is the concrete from which ideas are sculpted into reality.

When you are working with the energy of the Queen of Wands, you are harnessing the power of thought, ideas, creativity, expression, communication, and belief. When this power is flowing through you in a free and open way, you have the ability to open your mind. You have the capacity to embrace new ideas, without feeling threatened.

You have the capability to access logic and planning, while reserving space for potential that has not yet been created.

You have the power to express your ideas, and you are likely to feel cheerful, optimistic, hopeful, and youthful. After all, the strength of creativity and ideas means every moment brings the potential for joyful new beginnings. Who wouldn't feel optimistic?

This power makes it easier to get unstuck when trying to solve a problem, because the Queen of Wands is the mistress of creative solutions. Her gifts also make it easier to be outgoing, friendly, social, and communicative since she fosters your ability to understand other people, the natural world, and the spiritual realm.

Hers is the power of wit, intelligence, intellect, understanding, and language. Language is more than forming words and speaking; language is about expression and sharing energy. Think of our brains themselves, which have their own neural language of electrical impulses. Therefore, the power of the Queen of Wands is the power of energy flowing, opening to opportunities, creating understanding, and welcoming beginnings and expression.

Here's an example of a woman with a strong connection to the Queen of Wands: Brenda is a creative thinker who is great at trivia, puzzles, problem-solving, and thinking outside the box. She has a gift for languages and a way with words. When her friends need a dose of optimism or inspiration, they know to give her a call. She is always on the lookout for new opportunities and generally feels she can use logic and creativity to solve any problem. She is an excellent communicator and believes the most important thing in life is to learn and connect with others to create understanding.

The Queen of Wands Dethroned

Many circumstances can lead to energy imbalances. Life situations can diminish our connection to our energetic power source, but so can internal doubts, fears, and insecurities. These can grow out of critical feedback from another or from a project that does not yield the expected success. They can come in the form of disappointments, particularly those that disillusion us and cause us to feel disheartened. When an illusion is revealed, we can lose connection to the energy of our ideals. When we make a mistake or when a dream does not manifest, it can feel as if the Queen of Wands has been dethroned. This Queen also loses her seat of power when our minds work against our greatest good. An example of this would be pessimistic self-talk or beliefs that are based on doubts and fears.

We must all work to remain in balance, and sometimes even the most fabulous Queen loses her footing. When the Queen of Wands energy is off-balance or blocked, you may experience the following:

- ☑ Headaches

- ☑ Insomnia

- ☑ Anxiety

- ☑ Miscommunication

- ☑ Clumsiness

- ☑ Feeling flighty

- ☑ Forgetfulness

- ☑ Writer's block or other types of creative blocks

- ☑ Boredom; a lack of commitment/starting projects but not finishing them

- ☑ Intolerance of new ideas or others' opinions

- ☑ Pessimism and hopelessness

- ☑ Mentally "spacey" or overwhelmed

- ☑ Feeling ungrounded or "stuck in your head"

EXAMPLE: Our friend Brenda has been stressed. Having so many plans and projects in the works has left her little time to feel present in the moment. She has many social commitments and has recently noticed her excitement turn to anxiety. Since she has so much on her mind, she has trouble sleeping at night and is becoming bored with the outlets that used to recharge her.

Like Brenda, when you need to solve a problem but feel like you have examined all angles and still can't find a solution, or when you feel like there is only one option or only one solution to a problem, chances are your energy is out of balance.

Call on the Queen of Wands to nurture your mind, including giving yourself a break from overwhelming or racing thoughts. There is no danger in calling on this energy. As with all things, however, balance is important. For example, the Queen of Wands energy is great when you are learning something new and in student mode; however, if you are not balancing your energy, then perhaps when class is over and you are trying to sleep at night, the "student" in your mind is still racing around thinking about papers, research, and exams. Allow other aspects of yourself to be integrated so you can be at your best both day and night!

Have you ever known someone who was excellent at starting projects, but needed help finishing them? This is another example of unbalanced Queen of Wands energy. This energy craves the hope and inspiration of ideas and beginnings, but when not balanced, may grow bored easily and not follow through. Fortunately, energy can be moderated and that is exactly what getting to know your Inner Queen is all about.

Have you ever heard someone say, "I'm just not the creative type"? If you have said this yourself or heard it from someone else, then it is a good indicator the speaker has not met her Inner Queen of Wands. Creativity doesn't mean you must be a fine artist or a concert pianist. It doesn't mean you must be an inventor or a teacher. The energy of taking a thought or an idea and developing it until it becomes a reality is a creative act. Deciding to buy a house, and then buying it; choosing to decorate a room and doing so; resolving to write a letter, read a book, learn a language, or go on a vacation—whatever—all starts in the mind, and the power to envision is the power to create.

Connecting with Your Inner Queen of Wands

CREATIVITY

The following questions are intended to prompt your conscious awareness of the subconscious forces within that align with this Queen. Take your time, and have fun answering them in a separate notebook!

- ♛ What do you associate with the word *creativity*? What messages have you been given about your own ability to be a creative person?

- ♛ What activities help you brainstorm or feel creative?

- ♛ If your personal special creative power (and we *all* have creative power!) were represented as a fictional character or superheroine, who would it be? Remember, this is creative time . . . make it up!

- ♛ Are most of your ideas/thoughts/creative energies centered on one outcome or dispersed over numerous projects?

- ♛ What have you *always* dreamed of doing, if time and money were not factors?

- ♛ Imagine you are living your dream life now. What language do you use to describe yourself and your capabilities?

- ♛ What sounds do you hear around you in this imagined dream life?

- ♛ What does your space look like?

- ♛ What does an average day look like? What do you see around you? How do you see yourself? Journal or draw a scene from your dream life. Remember that by using your creativity to envision and commit this life to words or art, you are planting the seeds to make this life a reality.

- ♛ What stories do you persistently tell in your interactions with others? A story does not need to be mythic; it can be about the lover who got away, the unfair boss, a lifetime of bad breaks, and so on.

- ♛ What story would you rather tell? Surround yourself with the new story. Write the synopsis for your new script here and give expression to this new story every day. If told enough, the new story will stick!

- ♛ How is your breathing? What can you do to practice inviting deep relaxing breaths into your day? As you practice breathwork, envision the story you are creating, the new life you are dreaming for yourself.

Expand your energy by learning the language of symbols. Use your imagination to create meaning out of events large and small. Make your own symbol dictionary in the space below.

List any obstacles to manifesting your vision. Underline the three that are the most intimidating. For each, write a statement describing your plan to overcome this challenge.

- ♛ What interferes with your ability to think clearly and make decisions?

- ♛ What helps you develop ideas?

- ♛ Brainstorm any ideas you have had but have not yet had time to develop.

- ♛ Review your brainstorming list and pick three ideas that are most appealing to you now. Choose one of the three ideas and list resources that could help you make this idea a reality.

Inspiration

Make a list of people you find inspiring. Why are you inspired by these individuals?

Fears and doubts can cause us to lose connection to our source of inspiration. Without this lifeline, we become stuck in repetition and overlook opportunities that challenge our expectations.

When we don't believe a solution is possible, we are repeating doubts learned in childhood. Sometimes those doubts were voiced by others and reflect their own fears instead of our limitations. You do not need to inherit the fears of others.

Connecting to inspiring activities can help you achieve more success than insistently focusing on a problem from a strictly logical point of view. After all, logic is the best description of what you already know; inspiration is your connection to what could be.

Write out a plan to bring inspiration into your day for a time frame of your choosing. Plan to set aside time every day this week to practice inviting the power of inspiration and creativity.

Fill in the topics or thoughts you stress about most in the bull's-eye below. What topic is in the center, where you place most of your focus?

Imagine seeing your bull's-eye from very far away. What other beliefs, ideas, thoughts, or plans can be allowed into your mind to alleviate the stress on your target?

"If you don't like something, change it.
If you can't change it, change your attitude."
—Maya Angelou

Reality is a matter of perception and perspective. When you feel like you are in an impossible situation, use this tool:

Imagine your immediate problem(s) are in a bull's-eye like the one above. You are focusing all your energy on solving just that problem or set of problems.

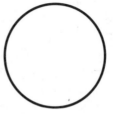

All the possibilities of the Universe are out HERE

Then, take a deep breath and imagine you are viewing your bull's-eye from far, far away. In the infinite space in the universe where all things are possible, solutions yet to be invented flow freely. From this standpoint, it is easier to recognize the existence of new solutions beyond what you can see in this moment.

The sense of sound also plays a significant role in creativity and inspiration. Create a music playlist of songs that uplift and inspire you:

_____

_____

_____

_____

_____

Communication can inspire or overwhelm. Inspiring words foster expansion. They uplift and create the sense that doors are open to you.

Explore statements that are "door openers," and notice what language you may be prone to using that cuts off inspiration. Words such as *not*, *can't*, *just*, *only*, or *but* can decrease the flow of energy to your goals.

Use the space below to create statements of inspiration and possibility.

_____

_____

_____

_____

_____

QUEEN OF SWORDS

Power of Passion

The Courageous Crusader

Passion • Power • Sensuality • Ambition

Meeting the Queen of Swords

After exploring the source of creativity, ideas, and inspiration (Wands), we now move into the territory of action.

The Queen of Swords rules passion, action, and the energy of putting ideas into motion. The Queen of Swords is also the ruler of motivation. Depending on the deck, she may also be called the Queen of Spades or Queen of Fire.

Have you ever been inspired to start something new, but then that idea passes and you move on to the next thought? There was no deep motivation to act on that idea, and so it does not come to fruition.

Many people spend their entire lives in this state of dreaming of plans and ideas, goals and fantasies, without summoning the motivation and passion to pursue these dreams. And without that impetus, no result will ever be realized.

Motivation is a double-edged sword, no pun intended. It is often associated with challenges and hardship because when we are most comfortable, we are also least likely to embrace change. Passion is stirred through the desire to experience something new or different from the status quo.

The Queen of Swords is the Warrior Queen with the fire and desire to call on her deepest motivation so she can employ the staying power necessary to go from thought to result. Her energy carries a powerful charge, and like the Warrior, she can be both a challenger and liberator.

When you follow your integrity even though it can be challenging, when you stick to your highest ideals and employ a strong focus to reach your goals, when you use the fiery power of feelings like anger to propel you into action, you are connecting with the Queen of Swords.

Many women are taught "good girls don't get angry" or that anger is bad and should be avoided. Conflict, however, can be a catalyst for change, justice, and improvements and bring beneficial results. The Queen of Swords helps women speak up for what they believe in. Her energy helps propel women into battle for justice, equality, and ideals. The Queen of Swords bestows confidence and assertiveness.

Use this energy when you need to have a difficult confrontation, when you need to feel more courageous, and when you need to communicate assertively. When you must stay focused on one mission, the Queen of Swords energy is just what is required. When you are in a slump and looking for your motivation and staying power, the Queen of Swords can help you spring into action. When you want to experience the pleasures of passion in relationships, work, or life in general, it is the Queen of Swords energy that will come to your aid.

When you are fighting for a cause or acting to bring justice to a community, yourself, or your family, this protective energy is also the energy of the Queen of Swords.

Sometimes conflict is productive, and the Queen of Swords helps you to embrace its challenging energy to really follow your mission.

Did you ever have a boss, mentor, or teacher who was considered mean or strict by others because that person expected a lot of you and held you to a high standard? Remember wishing that person would cut you some slack and give you a break? Then remember how amazing it was when you stepped up to the challenge, rather than backing down from it?

The power of transformation through overcoming obstacles is a strengthening, refining experience. This is the embodiment of the Queen of Swords.

Let's face it: we all appreciate what we accomplish when we must put up a fight.

The Queen of Swords also offers the energy of adventure, excitement, and risk. Her energy propels you to take a new exercise class, do something you are afraid of, or conquer an obstacle. Her energy motivates you to reinvent yourself, like the legendary phoenix, symbolic of rebirth and rejuvenation.

Hers is the energy of cutting through illusion to find the truth. She believes the greatest service she can give to others is to speak the truth, even if it hurts.

Here's an example of a woman with a strong connection to the Queen of Swords: Sylvia is a passionate woman who lives an intense lifestyle. She is drawn to situations and people who exude power and excitement. She is comfortable with her own power, but as a woman her behavior is not always accepted by others who are uncomfortable asserting themselves. She believes in speaking her mind whether others agree or not, and her friends know they can rely on her to be honest and to the point. Sylvia is not shy, especially when confronted with opportunities to bring about positive change. She has an intense personality and, when she is on a mission, can be focused to the point of obsession.

She detests boredom and doesn't mind rocking the boat just to keep some adventure in life. There are several causes that she feels passionate about, and she is not one to talk about change without taking action toward it. She loves to take risks and is always on the move.

The Queen of Swords Dethroned

Women are given mixed messages about power, confidence, anger, passion, and sexuality—all the things embodied by the Queen of Swords. Taught to deny feelings and drives, we are given complex rules to follow, dictating when and how we are "allowed" to express our natural passions.

It is no wonder this energy is out of balance in many women. We are rewarded socially for denying the Inner Queen of Swords and judged for following our passions. Even in the midst of a movement toward empowerment for women, there is still a lack of consistency in how society reacts to women who embody courage and determination. Thus, women are taught to suppress their inner fire and easily become detached from their Inner Queen of Swords, or they react against social standards and embody this energy in its ungrounded form, emphasizing this spirit but rejecting other forms of energy that are judged as too passive or traditional.

When the Queen of Swords energy is out of balance, you may experience the following:

- ☑ Power struggles

- ☑ Burnout

- ☑ Compulsive behavior or the compulsive desire to rescue others who are not ready to be rescued

- ☑ A need to take risks for attention

- ☑ Resentment

- ☑ So much focus you can't step away from an issue when you need to

- ☑ The urge to see people as either friends or enemies with nothing in between

- ☑ The desire to lash out at the world for perceived injustices

☑ The need to always be right or always have the last word

☑ Impulsivity

☑ Feelings of suspiciousness toward others or defensiveness toward others

Example: Sylvia feels comfortable with her confidence and power and often perceives it as her role to come to the rescue on behalf of those who have more passive energy than she does. She therefore has gotten herself entangled in power struggles with friends and colleagues that were unnecessary and at times enables others to remain in unempowered relationship roles because she enjoys being the strong rescuer. She is also becoming burned out because of the numerous obligations she has undertaken and her insistence that to ask for help would be showing weakness. She has become obsessed with her work and will often turn to abuse of alcohol to try to sleep at night because she is all fired up with excitement, anger, or both.

She has begun to alienate friends because she has lost sight of the occasional need to compromise and instead insists on being seen as right in every situation.

Hers is the energy of fire and, as such, can bring warmth, passion, and power, but can also become overwhelming and consuming. It is a vital energy needed to promote growth, but when this energy is out of balance, winning can become a preoccupation. You may find yourself burning bridges, so to speak. Power struggles can erupt, and the need to be right can surpass the need to find harmony and balance.

Have you ever met someone who loved to argue just to challenge the status quo? This is just one example of unbalanced Queen of Swords energy. Have you ever found yourself diving in headfirst to be a champion for someone less fortunate, only to realize too late the object of your rescue efforts did not really want your noble-minded intervention? This energy can cause us to put on blinders and only focus on the end result. When we fail to see the forest for the trees, this energy is out of balance.

When Queen of Swords energy is off-balance, it is hard to "look before leaping," and you may find yourself all fired up to take action before all facts are known.

Slowing down is a part of keeping the Queen of Swords on her throne.

Use the following to awaken the Inner Warrior. As you embark on your quest for the truth, keep in mind all energy has a higher purpose—even the energy you as a woman may have been taught to fear such as anger. The Queen of Swords is about action, so as you explore this part of your journal, you may feel called to move on aspects of your life that need a little spice!

Connecting with Your Inner Queen of Swords

PASSION

Make a plan to bring passion into your life today. You may take action toward a positive cause or get up and move to bring energy into your body. Movement puts energy in motion and stirs it within the body. Bring energy into action to overcome slumps. When you are feeling stuck, move!

♛ What are you most passionate about?

♛ If you were to crusade for a cause, what would it be?

Spend time doing what fires you up today.

> *"Grant me the serenity to accept the things I cannot change . . .*
> *The courage to change the things I can,*
> *And the wisdom to know the difference."*
> —Serenity Prayer attributed to St. Francis of Assisi

> *"The truth will set you free . . . but first it will piss you off!"*
> —Gloria Steinem

Anger is a natural defense to subconscious feelings of fear. It appears more powerful to get angry than it does to express fear, but if you look closely, you will find a core of fear behind expressions of anger.

♛ What are your biggest anger triggers?

♛ How do you handle your anger?

♛ How does this serve you/others?

- What, if anything, would you most like to change about how you channel your anger?
- What secret fears are hidden behind your anger?

Strength

Feelings like anger and hopelessness are often by-products of a perceived loss of control. When we are threatened by a situation beyond our control, we are often reacting to a script, a deeply ingrained set of beliefs about how things "should" be.

By changing the inner narrative dictating our sense of how life ought to be, we find the power to create new possibilities. Recall changing the story as part of the Queen of Wands exploration. By changing our internal dialogue of thoughts and how we describe events and our role in them, we exert a powerful impetus to transcend problems and challenges rather than be devoured by them.

- What activities make you feel your strongest?
- What do you perceive as the greatest threat to your personal strength?

How can you live in harmony with events beyond your control? What internal beliefs and scripts of yours need to be rewritten so that you can find power in your circumstances? Practice exploring, challenging, and rewriting your script below.

- What physical activities do you most enjoy?
- What physical activities or adventures would you like to try but have not yet?

Pick your top three most exciting activities. Make a plan to experience these adventures within a time frame that is reasonable for you—a week, a month, a year, or more. Make a solid plan to commit to this adventure.

- What areas of your life currently feel boring? How can you connect to your passion for crusade and action to spice up these areas of your life?

- ♛ How are you dealing with power in your relationships with others?
- ♛ Is this serving your highest good?
- ♛ If not, what can you change?
- ♛ How would you change it?

QUEEN OF CUPS

Ruler of Home, Family

The Loving Mother

Nurturing • Intuitive • Emotional • Sensitive

Meeting the Queen of Cups

The Queen of Cups is the ruler of love and family, romance and emotions. Your family may be bonded by blood or love, your children may be your progeny or your pets, but the ties that connect you to others emotionally are ruled by this Queen.

The Queen of Cups connects you to your heart center and all matters dealing with healing, love, acceptance, forgiveness, relationships, comfort, and emotions. She may also be called the Queen of Chalices, Queen of Hearts, or Queen of Shells.

The ability to empathize with others is an example of the power of the Queen of Cups. When you express feelings through laughter or crying, you are tuning in to the Queen of Cups. When you hold an emotional space for a loved one, you are doing the work of this Queen.

She is the archetypal emotionally nurturing mother figure. When you support another through your love and encouragement, you are calling on the Queen of Cups. When you listen attentively to the words and, more importantly, the feelings expressed by another, you are relating to the Queen of Cups. She also represents your own intuition expressed through the subtle communication of your emotions. When you listen to your hunches, you are honoring this Queen.

The ability to mother yourself and others is also the domain of the Queen of Cups. Have you ever known someone who treated everyone like family? Who opened her home and dinner table to anyone who needed a friend? Someone compassionate and loving without judgment? This person's energy emulated the energy of the Queen of Cups.

Here's an example of a woman with a strong connection to the Queen of Cups: Kara has always been very sensitive to the feelings of others and grew up mothering those around her, even at a young age. She has a successful career, but her greatest joy comes from her family, friends, and loved ones. She enjoys entertaining at home and is always nurturing others through her words or with food. She can't tolerate knowing others are in distress because she experiences their feelings as if they were her own. She is a true romantic and believes everyone should be given the benefit of the doubt.

Since she is so loving and compassionate, she will often extend herself to help others, and friends know they can call her at any time for support and encouragement. She is a great listener and will go out of her way to make sure others are happy and well cared for. Her biggest fear is that another will be suffering and she will be unable to help.

The Queen of Cups Dethroned

Many messages in modern society promote the concept that "It's all about *me*!" and this has caused a great deal of damage to the concept of relationships. The Queen of Cups energy loses balance when we neglect either our own needs or the needs of others in relationships. Either extreme ignores the true power of love to unite and connect.

It is also common for women to disconnect from their Inner Queen of Cups because they have been told their feelings are not valid. Women who perceive information intuitively often get messages from their peers and families that deny their instincts. "You're overreacting" or "you're too sensitive" are an example of the invalidating messages women hear that may cause them to tune out or doubt their perceptions. Sometimes women receive these messages from people who have something to lose if a woman were to trust her instincts; other times, these messages are attempts to soothe worries.

Women also disconnect from the intuitive power of the Inner Queen of Cups because this faculty is by its nature based on the power of feeling, and feelings can be overwhelming. When we perceive the feelings of others so strongly we become engulfed by them, it is tempting to numb the overwhelming emotions through alcohol, drugs, food, or an overinvestment in logic to the detriment of emotion.

Here are some examples of what you may experience if this energy is out of balance:

- ☑ Mistrust of others

- ☑ Enmeshment (becoming overinvested in others' feelings or choices)

- ☑ Feeling responsible to change others

- ☑ Feeling depressed or overwhelmed by emotions, belonging to you or others

- ☑ Codependency or enabling others out of a fear of abandonment or need to be needed

- ☑ Feeling like a martyr or like you must sacrifice to make others happy

- ☑ Forgetting to nurture your own needs or others' needs

- ☑ Becoming emotionally cold or detached

- ☑ Feeling unable to express emotions through tears, etc., or feeling unsafe with emotions

- ☑ Being overwhelmed by emotions

- ☑ Sensitivity to others' reactions and holding back out of fear of others' opinions or reactions

EXAMPLE: Kara has begun to miss meals both at home and at work because she has been tending to the needs of several friends who are experiencing difficulties. She feels obligated to try to ease the pain of others and, vicariously, her own pain that she perceives from those she loves. She then ends up compensating for her worry and her lack of self-care by indulging in junk food. She has been so busy nurturing everyone else she has stopped doing any of the things that nurture herself. She feels like a failure as a mother because one of her children is having difficulties that she cannot solve or prevent. She is becoming depressed and starting to dread hearing the phone ring because she does not know how to say no to others in need, yet feels absolutely drained and unable to be of any real help.

Have you ever met someone who was hesitant to acknowledge or say how she really felt because she was fearful about how others would react? Someone who was afraid to set limits with others or felt unrealistically responsible for other people? Perhaps this person went out of her way to protect others from the ups and downs of daily life, even at her own expense? This is the Queen of Cups energy out of balance.

Likewise, the person who tries to act like a robot out of fear that emotions will weaken her is also resisting her Inner Queen of Cups. The person who is afraid to be vulnerable in relationships or forgive, the person who is afraid to trust, is also not in touch with this Inner Queen.

When relationships seem unsatisfying or overwhelming, or when you feel detached from your feelings or unable to trust yourself or others, this is an indicator it is time to tune in to the power of your Inner Queen of Cups.

Connecting with Your Inner Queen of Cups

RELATIONSHIPS

Make a map or diagram of your relationships. Use symbols, images, and space to describe your network at work, within your family, at home, or out in the community.

- How do you define *family*?

- How do you express love for others?

- What dynamics have you been attracting in your relationships with family, friends, and significant others? What dynamics do you wish to change? How can you change your role in relationships in order to attract different dynamics?

Often, we are looking for love but overlooking the need to be loving to ourselves and others.

- How do you nurture yourself and others?

> *"People are often unreasonable, irrational, and self-centered.*
> *Forgive them anyway. If you are kind, people may accuse*
> *you of selfish, ulterior motives. Be kind anyway."*

> —attributed to Mother Teresa

- In what ways do you see your family or friends as an extension of yourself?

- In what ways do your expectations of others shape your view of whether you are loved or lovable? What signs of validation or approval do you seek from others?

- What makes you feel most emotionally secure?

FEELINGS

Feelings are not facts . . .

♔ Were you ever told certain feelings were bad or a sign of weakness? Were you ever made to feel guilty or badly for having or expressing certain feelings? Which feelings have you come to associate with weakness or loss of control?

There is nothing wrong with you. We have all been given mixed messages about feelings. They are normal. They come and go, and they are neither good nor bad.

♔ Have you ever been afraid certain feelings would overwhelm you or become permanent?

♔ Have you ever struggled to accept the feelings of another because they did not seem rational? What feelings in others are difficult to accept? Why?

♔ What feelings are most difficult for you to express?

♔ What feelings are most difficult for you to sit with and tolerate when you don't have the ability to change?

♔ How do you currently cope with feelings? How does this serve your greatest good? How would you like to cope differently?

♔ What is one thing you can do starting today to invite freedom from being emotionally overwhelmed?

Consider the role that visualization, ritual, or creative expression could play in helping you to release emotions.

Play with creating your own ritual to release emotional tension.

A ritual could be as simple as the act of bathing with the intent to release emotional sludge in the cleansing process. Being in or around water helps cleanse and connect to this energy.

QUEEN OF PENTACLES

Ruler of Wealth and Abundance

The Earth Mother

Patience • Abundance • Tradition • Grounding

Meeting the Queen of Pentacles

Modern women are confused by this Queen. The pentacle is not a symbol used conventionally these days in mainstream society. It has many connotations, but most commonly it represents the four elements of Air, Fire, Water, and Earth, plus the fifth element of Spirit, all combined to represent a microcosm of the universe.

Thus, the five-pointed star symbolizes a culmination of all potential building blocks of reality, surrounded by a circle as the unifying, encompassing force.

The Queen of Pentacles rules the force of manifestation: the power of matter, resources, money, health, and material abundance. In various decks her name may also be the Queen of Coins, Queen of Stones, Queen of Gems, or Queen of Diamonds.

Remember the Queen of Wands started this whole path with the power of creativity through the idea and belief? The power of the mind allows the birth of an idea.

The power of the passion of the Queen of Swords brings focus and refinement of that idea, plus motivation and drive to see it through despite challenges.

The power of the Queen of Cups adds the element of love, cooperation, and community, allowing others to help us do what we cannot do alone.

Finally, the Queen of Pentacles is the power of completion. She represents abundance as the end result of all these steps.

She is no more important than the others, as all these energies have their place and balance.

The Queen of Pentacles is the power of form.

Hers is the solid, enduring power of the shape of our success. When you create a painting, grow a garden, or raise a child, the energy may originate with the Mind, Heart, or Will, but the end result, the tangible, material form of your creative energy, comes from the Queen of Pentacles.

Hers is the power of money, abundance in all its forms, resources, the Earth and the harvest from the Earth. Hers is also the power of careers, as a vehicle for generating money as a tangible form of energy.

Just as communication is the vehicle to transport ideas (Queen of Wands), action is the vehicle to express passion (Queen of Swords), and relationships are the vehicle to transport love (Queen of Cups), money/tangible resources are the vehicle that transports the energy of value.

Thus, we express the energy of value in physical, concrete terms through the use of money or diamonds, gems, coins, or other tangible measures. The energy of abundance in the physical world is represented by the things we buy. This does not mean abstract things do not have value—they do of course! However, we have been taught to prove our values through purchasing power, through where and how we choose to invest our energy via work and how we invest our energy via money as well.

The popular saying "put your money where your mouth is" speaks to the emphasis on investing as a priority.

This is the territory of the Queen of Pentacles. Society has limited the scope of what it means to have abundance. We have defined value in terms of money, which is an efficient way to give form to an abstract concept. However, just like there is more to creativity than being an artist—as the Queen of Wands reminds us—there is also more to wealth and abundance than money.

Abundance and value are about resources, which include things like water, food, security, the home, agriculture, and so on. The Queen of Pentacles carries the energy of abundance and wealth that we are taught to express through our careers, money, cars, clothing, and other material products. The Queen of Pentacles embodies the energy of the stability, security, and the fruits of our labors, including the labor itself. Therefore, hers is also the energy of patience, hard work, and reliability.

The Queen of Pentacles connects us to our source of value and security, but we choose what we deem that source to be. If you are focused on the financial aspects of security, this is the Queen to call on. However, recalling another lesson from the Queen of Wands, we must at times think outside the limits of our small world if we really want to tune into the infinite power of the Universe, we can also choose to access the infinite energy of abundance and security that extends far beyond a new car and a paycheck.

The Queen of Pentacles carries the energy of value itself. Whether we value our work or our worthiness, we can appreciate what we have or who we are. Gratitude then is also a part of the domain of the Queen of Pentacles.

Hers is also the energy of patience and practical survival, and this energy connects us with the power of tradition and the past.

Here's an example of a woman with a strong connection to the Queen of Pentacles: Yolanda has always been reliable, trustworthy, and very hardworking. She understands money in a way others do not. She recognizes the long-term value of her investments, and rather than being impressed by fads, she manages her money cautiously and wisely. Her skills have paid off, and she can live comfortably but she is also very generous with others, as she recognizes it is her responsibility to contribute to building a solid community. Since she has an eye for value, she is not afraid to invest in material possessions that yield a high return either in promoting her health or the security of her family. She chooses her car based on safety features but also pays attention to style. Yolanda knows what tasks are worth doing yourself to save money and which are best outsourced. She has had a successful career as a businesswoman due in part to her patience, her ability to work hard and not let challenges scare her away, and her loyalty to her friends.

Yolanda honors tradition and will often be the last of her friends to make a lifestyle change even if she can afford to. Her greatest concern is providing security, and she does not take big risks.

The Queen of Pentacles Dethroned

The Queen of Pentacles presents a unique challenge. In order to truly understand the extent of the power of this energy, we must be open to seeing beyond the gratifying trappings of the material. Yes, her energy represents the material realm and is associated with the security we obtain from it, but her power is also a doorway to an infinite source of security and abundance that cannot be limited to the number in a bank account. If money were nonexistent, security and abundance would still exist. Likewise, if money were abundant, but there was no food to nourish the body, that money would suddenly seem useless.

Certain aspects of unbalanced Queen of Pentacles energy will sound very familiar. Our culture has not been good about bringing this energy into balance, but as individuals we can choose to be the catalysts for a new relationship with resources, abundance, and wealth by restoring balance in our own lives.

Many things cause imbalance here, but most common is social attitudes toward money and pressures that fuel financial fears. Money itself is energy in physical form, yet we easily lose sight of this. We come to attribute an inherent value to money that it does not have. Money only has value in comparison with material objects or, in some cases, segments of time. So we tell ourselves a new car is worth X amount of money and that a day's work is worth Y amount of money, but the money itself is simply a physical representation of the fact that one has worked or now has a car.

Even the things we buy with money become part of the illusion. The attainment of security through a career, money, a home, a car, or other material or financial processes feeds the myth that security can be generated and maintained and is within human control. In small ways this can prove true. In other ways, it is exposed as a part of the illusion. People who lose their homes to hurricanes or their jobs to recessions have the security illusion broken; however, most of us rely on the facade of security to feel comfortable in the physical world.

But even if material security is an illusion, it is not hopeless to say there is some value to attaining or investing money. When we work with money, we work with a representation of energy, and that has its uses. However, when our focus on the material becomes disproportionate and fear-based, leading to stealing, hoarding, or going to other unhealthy extremes, then we are out of alignment with the energy of abundance and into the energy of greed, all in the service of an ideal of security that does not exist.

So how do we get to feel safe? We can, for example, remember that regardless of financial or material security we create our own security by finding our own path to survival and abundance. Gratitude is one such measure, as is investing energy in building strong relationships, communities, and so on.

Unbalanced Queen of Pentacles energy may lead to the following experiences:

- ☑ Excessive fears about money, self-deprivation even in the midst of abundance

- ☑ Preoccupation with the material, compulsive shopping, hoarding of money, food, animals, or objects

- ☑ Deep insecurities or fears of not having survival needs met

- ☑ Difficulty being flexible and open to new ideas (The Queen of Wands can help balance this energy.)

- ☑ Isolation and the inability to ask for or receive help from others

- ☑ Losing our identity to a job title or career, feeling like work or money defines who we are or what we are worth

- ☑ Feeling a stronger personal connection to money or material objects than to other people or living beings

- ☑ Fear of change/holding on too tightly to traditions

- ☑ Struggling to compromise, feeling things can only succeed if you have your way all of the time

- ☑ Feeling sluggish, stuck or uninspired

EXAMPLE: Yolanda's business began to suffer as a result of the changing economy, and this triggered her fear of change. Rather than adapting to the times and evolving personally and professionally, she dug in her heels, becoming stubborn and ignoring the advice of friends and mentors. As a result, her business and net worth plummeted further. She convinced herself the solution was to discontinue charitable giving and hold on tightly to her money.

Yolanda can't bear to think of doing things differently than she always has and made some out-of-character risky investments. She lost a substantial amount of her savings and became disheartened with life, Spirit, and the world because of her circumstances. She tries to solve her problems by just working harder, but feels like she is swimming upstream.

Connecting with Your Inner Queen of Pentacles

SECURITY

What do you associate with security? How do you define wealth? Let's look at your expectations about wealth and security to see what roadblocks you may be throwing up in your own way.

- ♛ What were you taught growing up about work and success?

- ♛ What are your beliefs about money, wealth, and responsibility?

- ♛ What helps you feel grounded?

Now that you've explored your expectations about wealth and security, think about creating your own mantra about security. Mantras are brief affirmations that have the power to counteract negative thought forms that have taken hold of us through repetition. Mantras will work best when you believe what you are saying, so consider how to make yours realistic but empowering.

ABUNDANCE

"Expect Your Every Need to be Met . . .
Expect the answer to every problem,
Expect Abundance on Every Level."

—Eileen Caddy

Sometimes we believe that we value family, relationships, and health, for example. Yet when exploring how we are investing our time, money, and energy, we see our actions do not fall into alignment with those values.

👑 If your values and actions have fallen out of alignment, what can you do to change this?

List all the evidence of wealth and abundance in your life. Don't worry: You don't have to be a billionaire; wealth comes in many forms.

👑 For what are you most grateful?

👑 How do you use wealth to connect to others or to your goals?

👑 Are you holding back on investing in yourself or your dreams out of fear of scarcity?

👑 What is one thing you can begin to do today to feel more secure?

👑 What resources could you share with others? Create the flow of abundance into your own life by generating this energy on a daily basis.

Create space for new resources and opportunities by sharing what you have, by utilizing your resources with integrity and by releasing objects, items, and resources that are no longer useful to you.

♛ What beliefs about wealth or success sabotage your vision?

For any negative beliefs develop new statements to challenge them based on a world of abundance. If you are struggling to connect to abundance, review your list of evidence of wealth and abundance in your life.

We all periodically feel the strain of worrying about material security, including money. Here are a few ways to resolve this challenge:

♛ Make a gratitude list! Focus on and express thanks for the abundance that is flowing into your life!

♛ Share what you can. Invest time, money, or energy into helping others. This actually fosters a flow of energy and anything you can do to get energy flowing will help overcome a plateau.

♛ Remember energy flows in more ways than just the exchange of money. Volunteering time, bartering, sharing resources, giving gifts, cleaning out the house and donating items you no longer need all foster an open flow of energy allowing new energy to enter your life. You can also reconnect with abundance by spending time in a garden or in nature. The Earth, plants, and trees hold the energy of abundance and nurturing.

♛ In what ways do you share your abundance with others?

CALLING YOUR QUEENS

Now that you are familiar with the four powers within, it is time to focus on your ability to Queen Up and call on each of these Queens as needed.

Think of how simple it is to get answers from an internet search engine. Receiving guidance from your Higher Self/Creator/Spirit Guides is no different. All this process requires is intention, a request, and a willingness to receive. By calling your Queens you can align your energy with any of the four archetypal powers when you most need it.

Here is a recap of the Four Queens and examples of when to call on their energy. Remember, by calling on their energy, you are enhancing a part of yourself.

Queen of Wands—Creative Mentor

Opens the mind to ideals/potential

Brings inspiration and optimism

Encourages communication

Helps overcome creative blocks, feeds the intellect

Queen of Swords—Passionate Crusader

Brings confidence and assertiveness

Protects the disadvantaged

Pursues justice

Provides motivation to take action when needed

Queen of Cups—Nurturing Mother

Helps promote understanding/empathy

Builds personal relationships

Heals heartbreak and attracts love

Increases emotional sensitivity

Provides nurturing

Queen of Pentacles—Abundant Earth Mother

Provides grounding and stability

Offers security

Generates wealth/overcomes money blocks

Improves physical strength and health

The Process of Calling Your Queen

The power of intention requires more than a passive thought or affirmation. Here are the steps to call your Queen:

1. Find a quiet space to spend ten to twenty minutes in a comfortable seated position.

2. Close your eyes and focus your awareness on your breath.

3. Allow any thoughts or mental chatter to fade into the background.

4. Visualize the Queen you would like to call.

5. Invite your Queen to connect with you and to guide you.

6. Trust that your request is being answered, regardless of any results you perceive at this time.

7. Visualize how you would look, feel, walk, talk, act, think, and so on, if you were this Queen.

8. Allow any messages, symbols, feelings, thoughts, or impressions to arise without actively thinking. Open yourself to receiving guidance from your Inner Queen at this time and for the days to come.

9. Set an intention of honoring the strengths of this Queen in balance and harmony with the energy of the Universe.

10. Hold the image as long as you would like, and trust that you have gained the wisdom, insight, and power of your Queen. Be open to receiving any messages, intuition, or guidance throughout the coming days.

Steps 1–3 are basic relaxation/meditation techniques. It is Steps 4–10 that particularly call on your Inner Queen to work with you in a reflective or meditative state. Be patient with the process and practice it regularly to cultivate ease of shifting and honoring your power.

Overcoming Common Obstacles

TROUBLE MEDITATING

"I try to meditate but can't clear my mind . . ."

First off, forget the *m* word. Sit quietly with the intention to receive; that is all. If ten minutes is too long, try it for three minutes or even just two. Set a timer so that any preoccupation with the timing will not be a hindrance. Focus less on clearing your mind than on giving yourself permission to sit still, reflect inward, and allow thoughts without the need to monitor or talk back to them. With time and practice you will note a difference in how easy it becomes to turn the volume down on mental chatter and distractions. When I first began exploring meditation, I grew frustrated with not achieving my expected results. With time and guidance, however, I was able to get past this common pitfall. You have the ability to strengthen your meditative and intuitive skills as well. Remember, our modern lives bombard us with an overabundance of stimuli, so it takes some patience and practice to acclimate to stillness. Practice is key. You can do this!

COMMUNICATION BREAKDOWN

"I called my Queen, but she didn't answer . . ."

Communication through subtle energy is different from verbal communication. Your Higher Self/Spirit Guides are always communicating with you; you are just speaking different languages. Your language is literal: You expect words, sounds, and some body language thrown in for good measure. Your Higher Self/Spirit Guides use images, symbols, feelings. Be open to nonverbal communication. You may see colors, objects, or simply sense or feel something. You may pick up on a particular emotion or sensation in your body. You may suddenly experience a sense of knowing something even if you don't know where it came from. Take this as communication. Being receptive means trusting that what arises for you in a given session is correct.

ESOTERIC CORRESPONDENCES

A s you have learned, each Queen is the embodiment of an archetypal, elemental energy. Once you have called your Queen with intention, there are numerous complementary ways to invite her energies into your life to bring healing, balance, and the manifestation of your specific personal goals.

Whether you choose to wear certain colors to connect with the energy of a particular Queen or go all out and create your own personal ritual to work with the Queen energy within, the following section will give you the means to tap into the energies of each archetype.

Correspondences can be used to align with the natural cycles and seasons associated with each energy to enhance the power of the archetype. Remember, the energies of the Queens are found not only within us, but also permeate all of nature. Thus cycles in nature correspond to the seasons of our own life experiences, and we can consciously attune to this energy for a deeper, more empowered experience of our life path.

Correspondences also work to deepen our understanding of and connection to the presence of each Queen in all aspects of our lives.

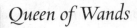

Queen of Wands

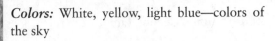

Colors: White, yellow, light blue—colors of the sky

Symbols: Wands, clouds, feathers, wings

Ritual Tools: Wands, incense, feathers, music, bells, or other musical instruments

Practical Tools: Pens, writing utensils, phones, computers, electronics, communication devices, books, publications of all kinds, arts, music, means of expression and communication of all kinds, the internet, fans, glasses, tools that improve vision, air quality and circulation, and the dissemination of information

Natural Element: Air, also wind, clouds, smoke, mist

Personal Power: Thought, creativity, communication, imagination, expression, vision, intellect

Emotional States: Joy, optimism, excitement, enthusiasm

Signs of Misalignment: Fear, anxiety, restlessness

Mantra Phrases: I see . . ., I believe . . ., I think . . ., I know . . ., I envision . . ., I inspire . . ., I create . . ., I begin . . .

Relationship Roles: Diplomat, optimist, cheerleader, teacher, mentor, guide

Heart's Desire: To create, to understand

Goddesses/Guides/Mythical Creatures: Athena (mentor in *The Odyssey*), Minerva, maiden goddesses such as Persephone, also those of the fairy realm, Pegasus, and angels in general, but particularly Archangel Raphael

Chakras: Throat (communication, listening/expression), Third Eye (vision), Crown (connection to Source)

Body Systems: Brain, nervous system, vocal cords, mouth, ears, head, eyes

Life Areas: Lessons, communication, expression, belief, perception of life and reality; academic, practical, or karmic learning

Zodiac Signs: Gemini, Libra, Aquarius

Time of Day: Morning

Days of the Week: Wednesday, Sunday

Season: Spring

Natural World: Birds, winged insects, rosemary, lavender, citrus, butterfly bush, flowering—especially fragrant—plants, leaves, quartz crystal, other transparent crystals

Balanced By: Queen of Pentacles

Queen of Swords

Colors: Red, orange

Symbols: Swords, spears, armor, fire

Ritual Tools: Swords, athames (cermonial knife)

Practical Tools: Flashlights, torches, lanterns, headlights, lamps, light fixtures, objects that illuminate, furnaces, heating systems, fireplaces, lighters, alarms, smoke detectors, vehicles, roads, knives, gardening shears; items that allow one to cut, remove, or dismantle; items that create heat or foster physical activity, protection, or alertness

Natural Element: Fire

Personal Power: Will, motivation, courage, passion, desire, focus, ambition

Emotional States: Courage, enthusiasm, indignation

Sign of Misalignment: Anger

Mantra Phrases: I do . . ., I will . . ., I act . . ., I charge . . ., I empower . . .

Relationship Roles: Protector, crusader, guardian, coach, disciplinarian, leader

Heart's Desire: To lead, to act, to bring justice, to protect

Goddesses/Guides/Mythical Creatures: Warrior goddesses, the Morrigan, Kali, Pele, Artemis, Ma'at, the Valkyries, Amazons and other warrior figures, dragons, Archangel Michael, salamanders, phoenixes

Chakra: Solar Plexus

Body Systems: Metabolic and endocrine, sexual organs

Life Areas: Lessons of balance vs. obsession/compulsion, those from which we derive power or status, sexuality, situations requiring focus and leadership, athletics, competitions, personal crusades, where we seek justice in life; how we manage authority, control, and dominance; ways we seek to purify, control, or transform

Zodiac Signs: Aries, Leo, Sagittarius

Time of Day: Noon

Days of the Week: Tuesday, Sunday

Season: Summer

Natural World: Tiger, lion, cat, birds of prey and other natural predators, reptiles, scorpions, gold, iron, lava, volcanoes, ash, sunflowers; any red, yellow, or orange crystals or stones such as citrine, garnet, ruby, red jasper, bloodstone; hot peppers, cinnamon, cloves, or plants with thorns such as roses

Balanced By: Queen of Cups, Queen of Pentacles

Queen of Cups

Colors: Blue, purple, turquoise

Symbols: Cups, ships, boats, shells

Ritual Tool: Chalice

Practical Tools: Any vessel containing water or liquid as well as water purifiers, bottled water, pools, spas, tubs, showers, plumbing systems, implements connecting us to feelings and empathy with each other, mirrors, reflective devices, any resources that allow for expression and sharing of emotion

Natural Element: Water

Personal Power: Empathy, love, compassion

Emotional States: Serenity, tranquility, love

Signs of Misalignment: Depression, neediness, dependency

Mantra Phrases: I feel . . ., I love . . ., I receive . . ., I embrace . . .

Relationship Roles: Nurturer, caretaker, mother figure

Heart's Desire: Connection with others, healing

Goddesses/Guides/Mythical Creatures: Sea goddesses; love and mother goddesses such as Venus/Aphrodite, Isis, Yemaya, Tiamat; Archangel Gabriel, mermaids, undines, nymphs

Chakras: Heart, Sacral

Body Systems: Lymphatic, uterus, breasts, digestive

Life Areas: How we give and receive nurturing, relationships, romance, family, pets, how we handle emotions, where we feel called to nurture or mother, listening to others, how we receive from others and from Spirit, where we are called to heal emotional wounds

Zodiac Signs: Cancer, Scorpio, Pisces

Time of Day: Evening

Days of the Week: Monday, Friday

Season: Fall

Natural World: Sea, bodies of water, dolphins, fish, sealife, turtles, otters, bears, seashells; blue stones such as lapis, pearl, moonstone, aquamarine, amethyst; most mammals and animals dwelling in or near water, willows, morning glories, lotus, lilies

Balanced By: Queen of Pentacles, Queen of Swords

Queen of Pentacles

Colors: Green, brown, black

Ritual Tools: Salt, altar, drum

Practical Tools: Furniture, home, tables, pillars, items that we rely on for foundation or support; all category of stones, brick, and building blocks; concrete, gravel, grass, mulch, soil, trees; banks, calculators and devices used to assess value; ovens, cookware and accessories used for baking as well as food, herbs, and seasonings; any devices that allow for preparation, planning, measuring, and storage

Natural Element: Earth

Personal Power: Patience, loyalty, commitment

Emotional States: Secure, calm, detached

Sign of Misalignment: Rigidity

Mantra Phrases: I trust . . ., I manifest . . ., I embody . . ., I maintain . . .

Relationship Roles: Businessperson, caretaker, maternal (practical rather than emotional), grounding to others, stabilizer, healer

Heart's Desire: To manifest, to grow, to secure

Goddesses/Guides/Mythical Creatures: Demeter, Baba Yaga and other crone goddesses, Gaia, Nephthys, the Goddess as Earth Mother, Archangel Uriel, gnomes

Chakra: Root

Body Systems: Skeletal, spinal, hands and feet

Life Areas: Where we seek security; work, finances, money, physical resources, also health and care of the physical body; traditions, values, what we invest in; home, food, cooking, practical comforts and luxuries; whether we allow ourselves to receive abundance, balancing giving and receiving abundance

Zodiac Signs: Taurus, Virgo, Capricorn

Time of Day: Night/Midnight

Days of the Week: Saturday, Thursday

Season: Winter

Natural World: Hibernating animals, moles, squirrels, animals who burrow or live underground, groundhogs, dogs, cows; most stones, rocks, and crystals but especially jet, obsidian, hematite; salt, plants; vegetables, especially root vegetables

Balanced By: Queen of Wands, Queen of Swords

BASIC RITUAL TO QUEEN UP

The most important part of any ritual is your intent or goal. Use this basic ritual as an outline for deeper work with the Queen energies. While an affirmation or meditation is a great way to connect with your four powers on a daily basis, think of a ritual as something you would do on a special occasion when you really want to bring yourself into powerful connection with one or more of the Queens. Just as you may have a daily self-care routine that is an act of self-compassion, but indulge in an extra-special luxury or treat on a particular day like your birthday, so too should your ritual working stand out as having an exceptional meaning in addition to your daily alignment practices.

Based on the knowledge you have gathered through the process of learning about the Tarot Queens, select a particular Queen you want your ritual to bring you into alignment with. For example, if you are looking for new financial or career opportunities, you would call on the Queen of Pentacles.

- ☑ Set aside time for your ritual in a relaxing space where you can focus undisturbed. You may choose to hold your ritual at a time that has significance to you as well or base your timing on the correspondences for the particular Queen you want to align with.

- ☑ Even though your ritual is focusing on one Queen, it brings balance to have all four natural elements represented, so include an object representing water such as a bowl, a candle representing fire, an object representing air such as incense, and another representing earth such as a stone. Be creative and draw on components of your culture, religion, or spirituality.

☑ Create a statement declaring your intention to cultivate a sacred space in which you feel fully protected and connected to Creator/Higher Self.

☑ Invite the presence of your guides/Higher Self and call upon the Queen aspect of yourself with the energy best suited to the goal of your ritual. Use the same process you use to call on your Queen in meditation.

☑ Employ all of your senses to focus on the intent of your ritual. See/feel/hear/sense the goal of your ritual as if the objective is already being accomplished.

☑ It is important to focus on yourself rather than changing others. In concentrating on elevating your own potential, rather than forcing situations to conform to your desires, you are empowering yourself as well as remaining open to potential beyond your expectations. Using the example of attracting new work, you would focus on awakening the Queen of Pentacles energy in yourself through connection with the correspondences listed above. You may, for example, surround yourself with coins, stones, or crystals. You may visualize yourself being confident, ready, and willing to embrace a new opportunity, and you may light green candles or employ other items corresponding to this Queen to set the tone for the ritual.

☑ Use a repetitive practice to build energy around your goal. Singing, chanting, drumming, rattling, dancing, repeating words related to your goal are some options. This will help you raise energy focused on the outcome you are seeking. Visualization is also an important part of this process, so see, sense, and perceive your goal accomplished.

☑ Always complete your ritual with an expression of gratitude for your guides and helpers.

This is a general template, so feel free to adapt the details based on your situation as well as your own belief system. Be ready, willing, and receptive in the days following your ritual. You have just sent a message out into the Universe; now it is time to be open and in alignment with that message, for your highest good.

Practical Ways to Queen Up

The tips below work to bring the energetic correspondences for each Queen into your life on a daily basis. Although they lean more toward the mundane as opposed to the ritualistic, they are nevertheless powerful ways to align your energy with the Queens. Above all else, intention drives energy. Practice the following not only as actions but as ways of focused intent to align with the specific energies associated with each Queen.

Queen of Wands

- ☑ Wear light, pastel colors from the correspondence list, and decorate with these colors as well.

- ☑ Use feathers to decorate or accessorize—feather pens are especially handy because this Queen deals with creativity, communication, and expression.

- ☑ Listen to upbeat, cheerful music or hang wind chimes around your home, office, or in your car. Listen to music featuring wind instruments. Better yet, make music yourself with bells, chimes, or wind instruments.

- ☑ Go for a walk someplace new and consider it a chance to explore. Bring your awareness to the smells around you, the sounds of nature, and the feeling of fresh air.

- ☑ Take out crayons and color, blow bubbles, or do other fun creative things that seem "childlike." Paint, draw, sing, create.

- ☑ Resurrect interests or hobbies from your childhood.

- ☑ Refresh the air in your home or office. Use essential oils or natural scents, floral scents, or plants to bring clean, fresh air into your living area or work space.

- ☑ Review your contacts list. Who have you not connected with in a while? Make a phone call, send a message, or write and e-mail to renew your connection to others.

- ☑ Play word games, challenge yourself with brainteasers, or explore new languages.

- ☑ Read a good book, write in your journal, or explore your creativity through writing.

- ☑ Create a special area in your yard, garden, porch, or patio—somewhere you can interact with nature. Designate this area as a place to connect with the Queen of Wands and her corresponding energies, including the energy of fairies (nature spirits). Place brightly colored, shiny objects as decorations or offerings, hang wind chimes in this area, or use other playful objects, such as pinwheels or other ornaments that interact with the wind. Flowers in this area will also enhance the energy and attract nature spirits.

Queen of Swords

- ☑ Wear red, or decorate with reds and oranges. Accessorize with objects that shine or catch the light like suncatchers, crystal prisms, and so on. If you are trying to decrease tension, however, balance this energy with the Queen of Cups or Pentacles.

- ☑ Use candles to set the tone and atmosphere. Red, orange, or yellow candles are ideal, but any candle will do. Decorative lights also focus the energy of the Queen of Swords.

- ☑ Listen to fast-paced, high-energy music. Set a playlist of songs that motivate you to feel free to dance along with the music.

- ☑ Exercise, especially in a way that challenges your comfort zone.

- ☑ Carry a token of your strength. Imagine this is a symbol of your power to assert yourself and protect your boundaries.

- ☑ Get involved with social justice causes or charities.

- ☑ Take a movement class, such as hot yoga, belly dancing, martial arts, or tai chi.

- ☑ The Queen of Swords is both a crusader and an activist, so blend these energies by challenging yourself to run your first marathon to benefit your favorite charitable organization.

- ☑ Make an altar or designated space for focused prayer. Use this space to connect with the energies of the Queen of Swords from the correspondence list. You can make offerings of ash from burnt incense, as well as crystals or stones corresponding to the Queen of Swords. Hers is the energy of power and motivation, so you can also create a collage of images, symbols, or pictures that motivate you and give you courage.

Queen of Cups

- ☑ Wear blue or turquoise and decorate with these colors as well.

- ☑ Surround yourself with ocean/lake/water images.

- ☑ Spend time in or near the water. Swim or play in the water when appropriate. You may even wish to leave symbolic offerings of love and gratitude to the energies associated with water. This can be a prayer, flowers, a blessing, stones, or expressions of your gratitude.

- ☑ Drink plenty of water, and remember as you hydrate that you are embodying the energy of this Queen. Also, the acts of bathing, showering, cleaning, and connecting with water in daily routines invite her energy.

- ☑ Listen to nostalgic music or love songs as well as meditation music featuring ocean sounds or rain falling.

- ☑ Use the word *love* excessively and generously.

- ☑ Cuddle with your lover, child, companion animal, or all three.

- ☑ Host a party and connect with friends. Practice giving and receiving attention and energy among friends and loved ones.

- ☑ Create a sacred space in your home to focus on immersing yourself in the energy of the Queen of Cups. This space can feature an altar or table on which you may place pictures or tokens of those whose love you wish to be reminded of. You can also decorate this area with flowers and expressions of self-love. Use this area to meditate and reflect on compassion.

Queen of Pentacles

- ☑ Wear greens and browns or decorate with these colors.

- ☑ Keep a budget. This is simply a record of energy in/energy out.

- ☑ Work in the garden or keep plants around you. Walk barefoot on safe yet natural terrain.

- ☑ Immerse yourself in a hands-on project, especially a home DIY project.

- ☑ Listen to traditional music from a culture or heritage you are interested in or identify with.

- ☑ Treat yourself to something that shows you your worth.

- ☑ Pamper yourself with special luxuries that appeal to your physical senses or help you care for your body. Massage or energy healing, scented lotions, comfortable clothing, nutritious food, and creating a comfortable space for work or relaxation are all ways to connect with the Queen of Pentacles, whose energy corresponds to experiences of the physical body and senses.

- ☑ Make a gratitude list.

- ☑ Create a sacred space in your home or garden where you can ground your energy on a regular basis. You may also create a special shrine or altar to connect with your roots by honoring your ancestors. Decorate this space with tokens from or pictures of your family and ancestors. Connecting with roots, foundation, and tradition aligns us with the Queen of Pentacles.

RECLAIMING YOUR CROWN WHEN LIFE KNOCKS YOU DOWN

By now you have learned that everything is energy and energy is changeable. We are more than physical beings; as an individual, you are a combination of various forms of energy, as well as a culmination of various past selves and even potential future selves.

Just as energy and emotions are always flowing and fluctuating, so too are states of mind, attitudes, and even our perceptions of reality. Since our perception of reality creates reality, even external circumstances are subject to change. When you experience a personal crisis, a loss, the end of a relationship, a health challenge, or the loss of a job, it feels like life has knocked you down. You may see the world as unfair, unjust, or have the impression that God, the Creator, or the Universe is working against you and your happiness.

Desires and longings can be compared to cravings. The ego aspect of ourselves wants to fulfill human needs and desires. Sustenance, love, comfort, happiness, material things, relationships, status—these cravings may be for basic needs as well as for things we feel will empower us, change our emotional states, and make us feel contented and fulfilled.

For example, Tanya, a successful businesswoman, eagerly awaits a new contract that she perceives will boost her business and bring her success, status, and an increased income. Her intention is to fulfill her business mission through this contract. On a personal level, her intention may be to bring abundance for her family through this business contract, to prove to her friends and family that she can be more successful than they give her credit for, or even to prove her own value to herself through this accomplishment.

Suddenly, the contract is not just about business as usual! When we stop to consider the subconscious desires and cravings Tanya brings to the table—the underlying meaning she has assigned to this business deal—we see how, like all of us, Tanya is prone to placing her validation and power as a person, the fate of her future, and her feelings about herself and the world into an external situation.

By taking an empowered view of this situation, Tanya could recognize that she has the energy to fulfill her personal mission of providing for herself and her family and satisfy her business mission through many potential opportunities in or outside of her chosen career and identity as a businesswoman and a woman about to make a special business deal. If Tanya were able to connect with the cravings behind this business deal, she would recognize how she is looking to the status and success of her business to heal old wounds and feel validated.

Once she connects to these subconscious cravings, she has the power to release beliefs, attitudes, emotions, and anything distracting her from seeing the reality in the present. She may or may not get the contract; it may or may not lead to anticipated success. Through this empowered stance, Tanya makes contact with her core sources of strength, power, and potential regardless of external circumstances. She knows that even if this deal falls through, she still has the creativity, intelligence, and communication skills to envision and collaborate with others (Queen of Wands). So she can create new opportunities and follow up with her powers of courage, ambition, and motivation (Queen of Swords). In fact, the same energy of the Queen of Swords will help her release obstacles on her path so that she is fulfilling her mission one way or another. She can tap into her power to find nurturing love and connection to others, unconditional love, and compassion regardless of her career status and heal old wounds that made her seek approval or validation from outside herself with the energy of the Queen of Cups. She would also realize that the ability to create abundance is not dependent on a once-in-a-lifetime situation but rather an ongoing opportunity. The Queen of Pentacles energy within her will help her to stay the course, be patient, get clear about what resources she needs and why, and generate an open flow of abundance energy that will come with this business deal or another better opportunity.

When we are at a crossroads in a time of personal crisis or transition, it is easy to get so focused on what has not worked according to plan or what has been mislaid that we lose sight of the regenerative power of the soul: the ability to recreate, reenvision, redirect, and regroup. To do this effectively, we must first accept and recognize our full sense of Self. In some cultures people believe that a trauma results in an aspect of the Self or the soul being fractured and left behind, as if a part of the individual stays in the trauma while the rest of the person moves forward, going through the motions and not feeling complete. Even psychologists recognize the way trauma can cause an individual to become stuck. Although theirs is the language of neurochemistry and not energy or soul, one could say they are describing the same process.

Shamans and energy healers use various tools to reintegrate the soul, mind, and body after a traumatic event or significant crisis. This can be helpful during times of transition as well. By integrating the Self, you are recollecting and calling forth the aspects of yourself, your energy, and your soul from all dimensions of your past. Think of this as an energetic process of taking stock of who you are, who you have been, and who you are becoming.

The familiar Charles Dickens character Ebenezer Scrooge goes through just such a process when the Ghosts of Christmas Past, Present, and Future bring him into contact with different aspects of himself in the story "A Christmas Carol." Similarly, by calling the aspects of yourself through the Four Queens, you are consciously and intentionally connecting with various facets of your own energy to bring healing and integration so that you can allow the best potential future self and optimal future life to emerge.

Here is an exercise to ask your Queens to bring your energy into harmony to heal after loss, transitions, and traumas. Feel free to adapt this process to your own needs. You may find that doing this exercise periodically is helpful.

Integration with the Queens Within

- ♛ Find a quiet space where you will be comfortable and free from distractions.

- ♛ Allow your eyes to close; sit or lie comfortably, preferably with arms and legs uncrossed.

- ♛ Allow distracting thoughts to float through your awareness without becoming entangled with them. Don't try to force thoughts out, just let them drift by.

☙ Notice your breathing, and as you follow your breath, notice that you are becoming deeply relaxed.

☙ Ask to be surrounded by the love and protection of your Higher Self and Creator/God(dess) directly. You may also ask your Spirit Guides to be present with you.

☙ Set your intention on the Queen of Wands within. You may see yourself or the image of this Queen appearing in some other way. Accept what you receive as correct for you.

☙ Ask that all of the aspects of yourself from the past, from past lives, from anywhere in time and space, be returned to you. That all aspects of your creativity and mental power, that all of your wisdom and knowledge of language and communication, that all of your creativity and inspiration be returned to you. You may feel or see or hear or sense that energy is returning to you. You may feel this energy coming into your head, coming through the Third Eye chakra between your physical eyes. Ask for all of the energy that belongs to you to be returned with the blessing of your Higher Power.

☙ Know that this energy is being returned clear of any negativity. It is being returned charged by the loving light energy of your Higher Power.

☙ When you are ready, repeat this process visualizing the Queen of Swords. Ask that all of your motivation, your confidence, your ambitious self, your sexual self, your confident self, and the aspects of you that hold your power, strength, motivation, and passion be returned from the past, from past lives, from anywhere in time and space, through the blessing of your Higher Power. Notice how you sense this energy returning. Notice that it may focus around the area of your Solar Plexus chakra below your rib cage.

☙ Repeat this process visualizing the Queen of Cups. Ask that all your energy from all time and space, past and past lives that is love, compassion, and healing be returned through your Higher Power, energized and cleansed of negativity. Set the intention that all aspects of yourself representing your capability to love and be loved, your empathic self and intuitive self, your mother self and child self, all be returned to you with the blessing of your Higher Power. Ask that all entanglements from fear or feelings of rejection or abandonment be released and cleansed now through the love of your Higher Power. Notice how this energy feels returning to you. Notice how this energy enters through the Heart chakra.

👑 Repeat this process now for the Queen of Pentacles. See yourself as the Queen of Pentacles. Set the intention that you call back to you the energy of your abundant, healthy, strong self. All aspects of yourself that are patient, loyal, sound, and secure are called back to you through the love and healing of your Higher Power, free of any negativity. All aspects of yourself from this and other lifetimes, that hold the power of abundance, security, and well-being are returned to you. Ask that any negative entanglements with fear or lack be released. Sense this transformation happening through the love of your Higher Power. Notice this energy returning to you through your Root chakra at the base of the spine.

👑 When you are ready, ask for the guidance of your Higher Power and Higher Self to create a path to health, abundance, inspiration, love, and courage. Invite the presence of your future Empowered Self. See how she presents to you; be open to any symbols, images, scenes, or words she has to share with you.

👑 Notice now how it feels to have your energy called back. Notice how there is no need to relive old scenes or replay old conversations. Calling the energy back to you is a powerful way to get out of the story of your old narrative and reconnect on an energetic level to create new opportunities in the future.

Part Three

52 WEEKS
TO QUEEN UP

YOUR YEAR OF EMPOWERED LIVING

You are now ready to build on the foundation of your awareness of the archetypal Queens and make harnessing the energy of the Four Queens an active part of your daily practice. This section provides techniques, resources, meditations, rituals, and more to help you work with the energy of the Four Queens for manifestation and intuition.

A Note on Attraction and Manifestation

We have discussed the Law of Attraction earlier in this book, and by now you have even used tools for manifestation such as affirmations with success. All too often, however, people eagerly embrace this concept of attraction at face value without understanding the mechanics behind it. Attraction and manifestation are ancient concepts now finding their home in modern western society. Practices of attraction and manifestation are based on aligning with energy to create a desired result, yet beliefs at the core of these practices are now blossoming in the midst of a culture that does not inherently support some of the basic pillars of this process. As a result, some people find the journey to attraction and manifestation riddled with distractions of the ego. Their goals do not come to fruition because they have only superficially embraced manifestation practices (which other cultures would call Magic or Magick, to distinguish it from illusion magic).

To use affirmations, for example, without strong intent and engagement in a practice of focused energy from a spiritually grounded mindset is to simply repeat words one hopes to come true at some later date. Manifestation work begins in the mind, so the words lack power if they are not backed with an emotional and energetic charge. Studies on consciousness have shown that when intentions are created, the power of affecting energy in and around ourselves is enhanced. We become proactive "programmers" rather than just passive receivers in default mode. The mechanics of manifestation require an intentional alignment of energy. This is not a matter of making a vision board and then covering it with refrigerator magnets and forgetting about it. It is not a matter of saying a few positive statements every day when all of your actions are out of alignment with your affirmations. It is not a matter of repeating behavior that is detrimental to your goal, all the while holding a picture in your head of what you really desire.

The above examples are reasons why many who have tried to work with the Law of Attraction have not been successful in manifesting what they thought they were aligned for. This is not attraction at all: It is wishful thinking.

To illustrate the confusion of this cultural intersection, for example, let's look at the example of Diana. Diana is open to eclectic spiritual teachings. Each year she creates a vision board, is careful to eliminate words from her vocabulary that are self-defeating, and uses tools like crystals to align her energy with her goals. She has felt frustrated for the past year, however, because she has been unable to attract a serious, loving partner into her life. She practices affirmations and has used various visualization techniques to see herself happily in love with her ideal partner, and she can't understand why these techniques have worked to help her manifest in other areas of her life but are not getting results when it comes to her relationship goal. Her mounting frustration causes her to back away from her consistent spiritual practices and lose hope in her worthiness as a person. She begins to believe that she will never find love and becomes increasingly isolated and sad.

What Diana doesn't realize is that years of modern conditioning have led her to expect instant gratification and to emphasize cognitive processes rather than integrating thought, will, emotion, and spiritual grounding. Her focus on affirming her desires as well as envisioning reflect society's emphasis on thinking, seeing, and asserting willpower (a combination of the Queen of Wands and Queen of Swords), and yet the energy is not being fully integrated through emotional and intuitive connection (Queen of Cups) or being grounded and rooted so it can manifest (Queen of Pentacles). Also, by putting so much weight on her own expectations, including an expected time frame, Diana is operating from the belief that her efforts need to bear fruit when *she* thinks she is ready. She has not, for example, accessed her Higher Self's wisdom to ascertain whether she is truly in a position to receive love and be open to a new relationship. She has not asked for guidance to ascertain what is blocking her or how to go about opening the doors in her mundane life so that a relationship can manifest. It is worth noting that Diana may have discrepancies between her affirmations in the mental realm and her emotions in the heart realm, also domain of the Queen of Cups. Her frustration and insecure feelings—as well as beliefs that if a relationship doesn't arrive by a certain time, then she is hopeless—have an impact on her energy vibration.

Now imagine that Diana has a deeper understanding of the relationship between intuition and manifestation and has adopted regular practices as a spiritually grounded routine. That is, she has a practice stemming from spirituality and a connection to a power beyond her own ego, extending to the Universe, the Divine, etc., as opposed to an ego-based practice focused on her desire alone. If Diana were practicing regular meditation and connection with her Higher Self, she might call on her Inner Queen to help her understand why she has not found the partnership she is seeking. Perhaps she would find herself connecting with her Inner Queen of Cups, and in doing so, accessing guidance to be open, go with the flow, and understand that there is greater healing still underway. Her Inner Queen of Cups may also reassure her that she will have a loving partnership. Perhaps her Higher Self can see that the ideal relationship is taking time to emerge because subconsciously Diana is resisting intimacy, keeping herself immersed in work, or isolating at home. Or perhaps her Higher Self would be able to communicate that new love is closer than she thinks. Her guides may have been showing her signs and signals all along, which Diana is not noticing because her expectations are too narrow. She has focused on projective, not receptive, energy. Even worse, because her own energy is impacted by her ensuing self-doubt and frustration, Diana may end up regressing from her path. This is akin to someone who, while driving to a new location, is convinced the journey is taking too long and, rather than checking the map, relies solely on what can be seen a few feet ahead. Not knowing where the path is leading, the driver becomes frustrated, turns around and heads home, not realizing the destination was only a few miles away after all.

Therefore it is important to check in to ensure that manifestation work is in alignment with your highest good, remain receptive to intuitive guidance as a counterpart to manifestation practice, and allow yourself to be open to the effectiveness of your will and its limitations in the larger scope of your life's journey. Also, it remains important to recognize the value of energy vibration that embraces the emotions and physical body, not just self-talk or thoughts that remain in the head.

Keeping affirmations restricted to your mind would be like expecting an electronic device to work when it has not been plugged in or turned on.

The following exercises provide weekly activities to charge your work with the energy of the Four Queens and aid in your manifestation process. Everything in existence is, at its core, made of energy. This energy has a vibration or pulse that may be imperceptible or invisible, but nonetheless exists. Furthermore, we can align energies to create a harmonic vibration. In a simple analogy, if two guitars were placed side by side and a D string on one guitar is strummed, the D string on the other guitar will also vibrate and both will create a sound.

When our own energy is vibrating at a certain rate, it can be effected by or effect the life-forms around us. Ever notice that when you are in a bad mood, being around two or three happy people has an effect on your energy? It will either lift your spirits or prove to be intolerable. Even in the case of feeling intolerable, it is a matter of your energy not harmonizing with the happy energy of the others. Therefore, you can either have an effect on or be affected by what is in your environment, without even being conscious of it! Recall the concept of thought forms in the beginning of this book—this section helps you delve into the process of recognizing, creating, or clearing thought forms based on your intention and intuitive guidance.

Manifestation and Modern Alchemy

Early scientists did not have a periodic table of elements, but instead recognized four elements from nature as the building blocks of all life. Air, Fire, Water, and Earth were considered the basis of all existence and were—and in some cultures remain—held in reverence as having direct ties to deities and other spiritual beings and forces. To understand a natural phenomenon, scientists sought to break down its elemental nature, and early medicinal systems classified humans as dominant in one of the four elements and their diseases as being an imbalance of the elements within the individual. Some practices continuing today are still based on this concept.

Therefore, to work with the energy of manifesting, attracting, or purifying (the basis of alchemy was not to create gold in the modern sense but to refine the Spirit from lead to gold), one had to understand the elemental forces at work both in the person and the environment. Thus, attraction had nothing to do with repeating a mantra, creating a vision board, or repeating happy statements, unless doing so would create an energetic attraction to the end result.

In modern society, we have become so pressured to get to the finish line that we inadvertently end up sacrificing the essential for the inconsequential. The Queen Up system is designed to provide brief, practical exercises to help you energetically align with what you want to attract without getting lost in the busywork.

Note, however, that it is the *intention* that should always supersede the action or words. Therefore, resist doing things like journaling for the sake of getting it done if you are not feeling what you are writing. In order to be in alignment, your intention must match your emotions, passion, and actions.

Use this section to create a system of personal accountability, reflection, self-improvement, and even spiritual growth at any time. What follows is a week-by-week guide to manifesting a life of purpose, balance, prosperity, and more. Tasks are given on a weekly basis, but go at your own pace. The exercises are numbered starting with Week 1, so there is no need to wait to get started to align with January 1 or any special marker of the calendar year, unless that is what you particularly want.

Each week focuses on the energy of a different aspect of yourself or your spiritual or life path as depicted by one of the Four Queens. The few exceptions focus on all Four Queens and an integrated self. As you progress through this planner, be mindful in your approach to completing each task; it is more important to act with integrity and intention than to finish early. These exercises are designed to boost intuition and aid in manifestation by working with the archetypes of the Queens through two channels. The Intuitive Channel requires receptive energy, and these exercises will ask you to be open to receiving guidance or information from your intuition. The Manifestation Channel requires you to project your energy as an active process. You will be actively engaging your emotions, will, and creativity to generate an energetic matrix for what you want to manifest. Any manifestation work should be done with a desire to cooperate with your Spirit Guides and Higher Self for the greatest good of all involved.

Remember the process of aligning energy requires a combination of intention, visualization, emotion, and action. Utilizing the meditations in combination with the weekly exercises is the basis for manifesting the results you desire.

Ready to practice? Are you ready to Queen Up?

WEEK 1

Envisioning the Future

The Queen of Wands rules our powers of creativity, inspiration, and visualization. To create a vision of your ideal path ahead, call on this aspect of your energy. Don't worry about how you will accomplish creating this future life or become this future self. For now, focus instead on imagining the vision and holding this image in your mind. Align with the Queen of Wands within to connect you to the creative well of inspiration as you explore the details.

Where would you like to be in six months?

In one year?

In five years?

Remember, envisioning does not commit you to anything. This is your creative playground, and you can change your mind at any time. By exploring your fullest potential, you are allowing yourself to push beyond limitations and boundaries. Give yourself the freedom to let your mind wander and visualize what you would like to call forth in your life in the next six months, year, or five years. You may also choose shorter time frames if you wish.

Read all the following steps prior to engaging in this meditation. This template may be followed exactly, or you may choose to elaborate on the steps. Trust the process and allow yourself to experience this exercise through all of your senses.

Queen of Wands Meditation to Envision the Future

♛ Give yourself time in a quiet space and allow your breathing to slow and deepen.

♛ As your breathing becomes more natural and relaxed, allow distracting thoughts to fade quietly into the background.

♛ Set an intention that you are calling forth your Inner Queen of Wands.

- Take a moment to allow the power of creativity, inspiration, intellect, communication, and big vision to arise from within you.

- Notice how this energy feels. What colors or sights do you see? What sensations do you feel in your body?

- Sit with the essence of the Queen of Wands for a moment, and when you are ready, ask her to show you what could be possible, in alignment with your highest good, in six months (or your own designated time frame).

- Free yourself from judgment as you trust the Queen of Wands within. She can see farther than you and uncover more of your potential than you may be aware of.

- Take in the vision she gives you.

- What does this future best potential for your highest good look like? What do you see around you? What sounds do you hear? What smells, sensations, and emotions do you notice? What do you see yourself doing more of? What do you see yourself doing less of?

- Ask your Inner Queen of Wands to open your mind to the words that will guide you on this path to your highest potential. Take a moment to receive the words or phrases she shares with you. Remember, you may hear these words or sense them or see images of or scenes conveying her message to you. Remain open-minded.

- Notice any place in your body that feels tense or where you feel constricted or restrained. Without judgment, imagine your breath moving into these parts of the body and carrying away the tension as you exhale and invite your body to relax.

- Spend as long as you would like with this image of your future self, living this ideal future life.

- If thoughts about how to get there arise, breathe into the scene on a deeper level and release these worries. Remind yourself that you are being guided toward this goal and the tools will be shown to you when it is appropriate.

👑 When you are ready, thank your Inner Queen of Wands for guiding you and awakening this vision.

👑 Gently allow your eyes to open.

Use the space below to take note of your experience. Practice this meditation each day this week. Notice any changes that unfold with each session.

Week 2

Queen for a Day

Build on your vision of an ideal future from last week and write a story about a day in this new life.

Begin by aligning with the Queen of Wands to focus your power of creativity through the written word. You may repeat the Queen of Wands meditation, or you may simply find a quiet place to sit with your journal and invite the Queen of Wands within to be present with you. Take a moment to sense the shift in your energy as you feel yourself connecting with the power of creativity, communication, and vision. You may perceive her as a guide, as a part of yourself, or physically as sensations in your body or a presence with you. If you aren't sure if you are making the connection, bring to mind an image you associate with a creative, inspiring power of the mind and hold this image for a moment before proceeding. Trust that you are making the connection.

From this place of alignment and flowing creative power, you are ready to create the story of a day in your future life or from the standpoint of your future self. Bring as much detail as you can into your story.

When do you wake or go to bed? What do you see around you when you first open your eyes in the morning?

What do you eat?

Who is around you?

What do you do to take care of yourself?

What activities do you prioritize?

How do you feel?

What do you hear around you?

What do you think on an average ideal day?

What words do you use? What words do you not hear around you, or what words do you no longer say?

Who are you close to?

What is your source of play?

What is your mission and how do you fulfill it?

Play with this exercise and most importantly be creative and have fun with the process. This is your ideal—as if you were Queen for a day.

When you are finished, read your story to yourself. Underline or highlight any aspects of your story that could be integrated into your present life. How could you blend these aspects of your ideal life? How can you begin creating this ideal life today?

Each day this week return to your story. This time, instead of focusing on the future, write the ideal day you are about to have. Write this story from a place of gratitude, expressing thanks for the outcome you are about to enjoy. Trust the process, and remember to connect to the power of the Queen of Wands within in each practice.

WEEK 3

A LETTER TO YOUR FUTURE SELF

Take a moment to align with the Queen of Wands. Having practiced this process, you may find that you are recognizing her energy sooner or feeling a stronger connection.

Today's writing focuses on the connection between your future and present self. Write a letter to your present self from your ideal future self.

If you feel anxious about anticipating what your ideal future self would say, take a breath, relax, and remember this is all about the process of connecting with your imagination and power of creativity. Creativity is your capacity to create, bringing something from nothing, so start with an idea and allow the process to unfold.

Here is a template, but feel free to stray from this outline and make it your own.

Dear Present Self,

I wish you could see the view from here! It is spectacular! I am so grateful to you because I am surrounded by _____. It is so rewarding to live a life of _____. Thank you for your bravery in creating the foundation for the life I get to enjoy. My favorite parts of this life are _____. I remember how stressful it used to be, when you worried about _____, or thought _____ would never happen, but I can assure you, _____ is possible and worth the effort. If there is one burden I would love to see you release it would be _____. Trust me, you don't need to carry this anymore and you will be so much better off without that stress. I know you sometimes fear _____, but everything works out better than you could have expected, next time you are afraid of _____ just remember me telling you that when all is said and done you have a great life filled with _____, _____, and _____.

The biggest lesson you need to focus on right now is _____. I promise you, you will be able to work through this and the benefits are going to be amazing!

I can't wait until you get to see the fabulous things in store for you, such as _____, _____, and _____.

Sincerely,
Your Ideal Future Self

As always, go with the flow and allow the energy to carry you.

For the rest of this week, make time daily to reflect on the wisdom from your future self, integrating her advice and lessons into the present.

Week 4

Get Fired Up

Time to bring in some action so that your beautiful vision becomes reality! The Queen of Swords within you is ready to light a fire of passion so that your dreams flow from your mind into your Solar Plexus chakra—the home of will and confidence!—and generate the energy for you to create the life you desire.

Now that you have spent some time with your ideal future image of your life/yourself, make a list of the elements of your future lifestyle. Think of that lifestyle as the routines, activities, priorities, and habits to which you devote your energy. Your lifestyle is the culmination of your ideals in action. For example, if your ideals involve family and quality time, yet your lifestyle involves working around the clock and very little socializing with your family, then an adjustment is needed.

Hold the sense of your ideal future life in mind as you connect this week to the Inner Queen of Swords.

Call on the Queen of Swords within to connect with the power of passion, confidence, motivation, and focus and the capacity to step into action to create the results you desire. Imagine the Queen of Swords as an aspect of yourself or as a guide.

Use all of your senses to connect with her: See her, notice what sounds you associate with her, pay attention to what physical or emotional sensations in your body connect with her energy, and so on. Feel a surge of warm energy rising from your Solar Plexus chakra in the center of your body below your rib cage and above your navel.

When you are ready, make a list of actions you can take in the present to create your future life. It is okay to start small. Make a list of steps you can take and practices and habits that you can use to add focused energy to your dreams and ideas. Through these actions, you bring your dreams to life.

For example, if your future self in your ideal lifestyle is social, outgoing, and assertive, begin practicing presenting yourself in this way, even if you have to "fake it 'til you make it" at first. Try it out!

As another example, if your future self wakes up earlier, meditates in the morning, and then goes to the gym before work, make a plan to bring these activities into your life starting now.

Don't just set up the plan, however, put that plan in motion!

Let your Inner Queen of Swords spark the light of motivation for you.

Her energy is great for action, focus, and discretion. If you can't bring on all the changes at once, that is fine. Pick one and begin with that, but action is essential.

My plan for this week is _____.
(Be specific. Rather than saying "exercise," spell out the details as in "Wake up at 6 a.m. and work out on the treadmill for 40 minutes," and so on.)

WEEK 5

TRUST YOURSELF

How are you doing so far? Did you make commitments to yourself and follow through?

Trust issues begin at home. If you can trust yourself first, you can extend that trust others because you know you have made a personal commitment to protect your integrity by following through on your promises. Yes, even your promises to yourself are important. By making a promise to yourself and keeping it, you are starting to heal trust issues in all your relationships.

Revisit your action commitments: What are you committed to changing starting today? Part of integrity is following through, so be fair to yourself. Make a reasonable expectation, not an impossible list of things to do.

Use the template that follows on page 94.

Commitment 1

Action: _____

What I hope to achieve by doing this: _____

_____

Why this is so important to me: _____

_____

Potential barriers: _____

_____

Plan for overcoming potential barriers: _____

_____

Commitment 2

Action: _____

What I hope to achieve by doing this: _____

_____

Why this is so important to me: _____

_____

Potential barriers: _____

_____

Plan for overcoming potential barriers: _____

_____

Commitment 3

Action: _____

What I hope to achieve by doing this: _____

_____

Why this is so important to me: _____

_____

Potential barriers: _____

_____

Plan for overcoming potential barriers: _____

_____

WEEK 6

ABUNDANCE & GRATITUDE

The Queen of Pentacles represents our potential for abundance, as well as the physical manifestation of our dreams and desires. As hers is the energy most easily associated with the physical realm—be it the physical body or the embodiment of energy as money, wealth, and material objects—she also represents the flow of energy into those things we value.

One of the simplest ways to immerse yourself in the energy of abundance is to express gratitude for your current harvest.

Make a gratitude list each day this week. Try to schedule this first thing in the morning or before going to bed at night. How are you doing on your commitments?

WEEK 7

HOW ARE YOU FEELING?

Emotions are the language of the Queen of Cups within. She communicates with you through your feelings and sensations. The fast pace of modern life provides an easy distraction from emotional signals. At best, we tend to treat emotions as an inconvenience to be silenced or ignored. When we allow that, we are missing essential opportunities to receive important communications from our bodies and Higher Self. Emotions flow and change, and we have much to gain from sitting with them and letting them surface.

Often, we confuse the need to sit with emotions and the desire to react to them. This week is all about recognizing and being present with your various emotions, without feeling the need to respond to or change them.

- ♛ Set a timer on your phone or another device each day this week. Make the times random throughout your waking day, or regular, such as every three or two hours.

- ♛ When your timer goes off, stop what you are doing, close your eyes and breathe a clearing, relaxing breath.

- ♛ Bring your attention to your Heart chakra in the space in the center of your chest.

- ♛ Imagine your Inner Queen of Cups emerging before you. Envision her as a part of yourself or as a guide.

- ♛ Feel her connection to your Heart chakra. Invite her presence to be clear and strong and sense her energy.

- ♛ Allow yourself to connect through your Heart chakra with your present feelings.

- ♛ Free yourself from judgment, expectations, and rationalizations. Simply allow the presence of the Queen of Cups within to bring emotions you are experiencing to your awareness through your Heart chakra.

- ♛ Ask your Inner Queen of Cups, "What does my heart need most right now?" Listen for the answer. It may come in images, feelings, sounds, words, or other sensations.

Practice recognizing the emotions present when your timer goes off. Notice how they change and where in your body they reside. You can even ask what they are trying to show you.

Practice this exercise several times each day this week. You may choose to write down your observations as an emotion log, or you may decide to notice emotions as an observer from session to session.

WEEK 8

INCUBATING YOUR DREAMS

Keep tuning in to your heart throughout the day this week without setting a timer. Practice making this a natural part of your day.

Go back and reread your initial ideal future self/ideal life description from the beginning of this process. Does this vision still resonate with you? It is okay to change course! Give yourself permission to shift focus or to realign with the ultimate vision of your dream life. As you sit with your ideal vision for the future, bring your awareness into your Heart chakra and ask if this vision resonates with you on an emotional level. Release expectations and fears and notice what arises. If you feel that your mind desires a certain outcome but your heart is not in alignment with that, invite your Inner Queen of Wands and Inner Queen of Cups to join you in meditation. Ask their guidance to determine the best outcome.

For example, you may ask, "Why does this not resonate with me emotionally?" Notice the signals you receive. Are you feeling fear? Is your vision serving a limited ego need more than the higher good of your mind, body, and spirit?

Be patient with yourself as you allow the assistance of your Inner Queen energy in resolving any discrepancies you may feel. If fear is a barrier, ask what the fear is teaching you. Are you ready to pursue this path? Are you becoming overwhelmed?

The Inner Queen of Cups is the energy of the nurturing mother. Let yourself be nurtured as you incubate your dreams for your future self and ideal life.

If your heart and mind are in alignment, reflect on enjoyable, satisfying things you can do this week to bring this future life into manifestation. How can you nurture yourself in the present to support the manifestation of this future life?

Week 9

Love Notes

Write three love notes each day this week. They can be to anyone you choose. There are only two rules:

1. You have to write one to yourself each day.

2. Love notes written to others must be sent to them.

Call on the Inner Queen of Cups to help you express love for yourself and others. Remember love is not limited to romantic relationships. Give yourself permission to express the unconditional love, gratitude, and admiration you feel for the important people in your life, including yourself!

Week 10

Lighting Your Spark

Motivation check-in: How are you managing your commitments to yourself?

What changes are you noticing in how you feel, your lifestyle, or how you see yourself?

Work with your Inner Queen of Swords, as the power of passion and the Courageous Crusader within you give you the strength to stick to commitments and manifest your vision.

Queen of Swords Ritual for Focus and Commitment

This is a simple ritual and can be performed in any quiet, private space. For this ritual you will need a red candle, paper, and a pen. You may use your Inner Queen of Swords card as well.

- First, take a moment to call forth the energy of the Inner Queen of Swords.

- Sit with your eyes closed and notice your breathing.

- With attention on your breathing process, notice that it is comfortable and easy to take slow, natural, full breaths.

- Visualize stress, unneeded distractions, or energy baggage being released with every exhale.

- Visualize empowering, radiant, warm, invigorating, vital energy coming into your body with every inhale.

- Repeat this process for three to six cycles. You may ask for the guidance and presence of any significant spiritual beings, deities, guardians, guides, etc. Invite their protective, loving energy to surround and envelop you.

- See yourself surrounded by a protective white bubble of energy.

- Visualize your Inner Queen of Swords as an aspect of yourself or a guide who is with you.

- Open your eyes, and ask for the help of your Inner Queen of Swords as you write your goal on your paper. Beneath the statement of your goal, practice writing one sentence of focused commitment. Write it again and again as often as you need to in order to create a concise, focused declaration. For the best results, write this statement as an outcome, not as a desire. For example, it is stronger to say "I successfully run the Boston Marathon" as opposed to "someday I will successfully run the Boston Marathon" or "I want to successfully run the Boston Marathon."

- Rather than crossing out any "mistakes," simply rewrite your declaration until you have pared down your exact intention and commitment.

- Now light your red candle, and place the Queen of Swords card below the candle. Hold the paper with your intention between the palms of both hands.

♛ Focus on the candle flame. As you watch the flame, envision the fire giving you strength, courage, and determination.

♛ Imagine the flame sparking your motivation. You may even feel the fire rising within you and adding passion and motivation.

♛ Visualize your Inner Queen of Swords cutting away any distractions and easily and effortlessly piercing any obstacles or barriers to clear a path for you to succeed.

♛ As you continue to focus on the flame, envision your own personal energy and all of the places in which it has been scattered. With each breath, visualize your energy flowing easily into the center of your core, into your Solar Plexus chakra.

♛ Now as you breathe and focus on the flame, feel this energy rising up through your body. This energy forms a stream that flows through both your arms, and into both your hands surrounding the paper with your intention written on it.

♛ This current of energy continues to rise up into the center of your forehead to your Third Eye chakra.

♛ As you continue to breathe and focus on the flame, imagine your energy, now centered on your Third Eye, as a laser beam. Perhaps it is red—perhaps white—or whatever color appears to you.

♛ Now project this energy laser beam out from your Third Eye. Envision that energy continues to flow from the candle, to your Solar Plexus, up to your Third Eye, and out before you where it is creating the energy matrix for the goal you wish to manifest.

♛ Imagine that through this cycle of energy you are feeding power into the process of creating your future goal, completing this goal, and adding powerful focus and will.

♛ Set the intention that the fire within you is easily charged, fueling your motivation, courage, and focus and bringing your goal into manifestation. See this manifestation occurring.

- Speak your intention and goal out loud three times.
- Speak your commitment to yourself to continue to fuel this goal three times.
- Assert that you will collaborate with your Higher Self, Higher Power, or Spirit Guides in this endeavor if it be for the highest good of all involved.
- When you have finished this ritual, spend a few moments drawing up additional energy for yourself, so that your momentum carries over for the days ahead.
- Thank your guides and the Inner Queen of Swords for aiding you in this process.

You may repeat this ritual daily until your candle has completely burned down.

Week 11

Desire Week!

What do you desire? Make a Desire List below and include not only *things* that you wish for, but also feelings or states of mind.

Review your list and pick your top three desires. Then treat yourself to the experience of fulfilling these desires to the best of your ability. For example, if you desire a vacation but are on a tight budget, create a vacation experience within your means that fulfills the desire you have—for relaxation, a change of scenery, pampering, etc. Practice fulfilling at least one desire every day.

Week 12

Service

How did it feel to realize your desires last week?

Desires are connected to the realm of the Queen of Swords. When we are focused on getting our own desires and needs met, we naturally set more boundaries, clear distractions, and show greater stamina and perseverance. When out of balance, however, this energy can tip the scales in favor of self-focus to the exclusion of considering the needs of others. Thus, this week we will balance the intense energy of the Queen of Swords with the compassionate energy of the Queen of Cups.

With her connection to the Water element, the Queen of Cups balances out the heat of the fiery Queen of Swords and also tempers any focus on self with a focus on others. Ultimately if we are to achieve our goals, it is best to do so in a way that serves the highest good for others as well. Numerous books on business success emphasize the importance of being of service in the process of getting your own needs met. This upholds the equilibrium between giving and receiving in relationships.

This week notice the desires others bring to your attention. What do your friends, family, coworkers, or even strangers express as their desires? How can you help the energy flow toward the manifestation of their wishes? This does not need to be a matter of giving financially. Look deeper into what is expressed. Does someone long for an hour of your energy and undivided attention? Do you have a skill or talent that could fulfill a desire of someone who needs help?

Give your energy in service to fulfilling the desires of at least one person every day this week.

WEEK 13

WATCHING THE FLOW OF ABUNDANCE

Make a special financial journal to be used to track your spending and income. This is not a budget, but a ledger for more than just accounting purposes:

You are tracking the flow of abundance.

Doesn't that sound much sexier than "where I spent my money and how much I earned"?

Track the flow of physical abundance energy by keeping a list of income and expenses, but the purpose is being able to see proof of abundance in your life.

If you are afraid to look, relax, release your expectations, and remember there is no better way to get a handle on any behavior than by looking at the big picture and keeping a record.

WEEK 14

QUEEN OF PENTACLES, YOUR PERSONAL ACCOUNTANT

Call on your Inner Queen of Pentacles for assistance empowering your finances. Here are some tips to power up your pocketbook with the energy of abundance.

Your Personal Shopper

Before making purchases this week, take a moment to close your eyes, breathe, and envision your Inner Queen of Pentacles. From this place of being centered and connected to the energy of values and abundance, ask your Inner Queen if this purchase is for your highest good and whether this is the time, place, and price that will best suit you. Notice the response you receive, even if it surprises you. Remember you ultimately have the final say in your choices and actions. Simply notice when you follow this guidance and what the outcome is.

If you feel a "no" response, ask if there is a better option if this is not the optimal time, place, and price. If the purchase feels important to you, ask for guidance finding ways to get this need met by an alternative route. For example, if you feel like you need to purchase a new laptop but your Inner Queen of Pentacles is guiding you to hold off on making the purchase, ask for direction on creating the opportunity to get your need for a laptop met. Perhaps there will be a sale the next day, or perhaps a friend is about to give you one. Be open to possibilities you aren't expecting.

Divine Budgeting

When you work with your Inner Queen of Pentacles, a budget is more like a ritual or a prayer than boring bookkeeping. Ask for the guidance of your Inner Queen of Pentacles, and in your notebook or spreadsheet, establish your typical budget categories for regularly occurring expenses. Save a category for goals such as a vacation or a new car and emergencies.

Now, as you begin to fill in the numbers, rather than focusing on the lowest possible way to meet each need, focus on what amount would adequately satisfy your comforts and needs. Be realistic but flexible. Rather than shortchanging yourself by always aiming low, invite your Inner Queen of Pentacles to provide you with insight into what areas will need more energy/money this month.

Thus, you are not only doing a little budgetary divination, but you can also invite the energy of abundance into your budgeting. Rather than thinking, "Oh, no! I am going to be spending $300 on groceries!" focus on the energy of abundance. Say to yourself, "I will easily attract the opportunities to invest $300 in groceries so that I can feed my body healthy, nutritious foods."

Repeat this for each category, from the mind-set of abundance instead of expense.

Sharing the Wealth

The next time you write a check or make a donation to your favorite charity, align with your Inner Queen of Pentacles and take a moment to cultivate the energy of abundance and growth. As you feel stability and security blossoming all around you, envision that you are also sending this energy to the charity or organization through your donation. Visualize your generosity as a seed that is planted, growing, blooming, and spreading, creating abundance and stability for the benefit of your community and the world around you.

Setting Roots for Abundance

If you feel overwhelmed by career or financial demands, or if you want an easier flow of income, resources, and financial energy in your life, use this exercise to open your energy to the flow of money and resources. Most importantly, this exercise protects your most valuable physical resource: your body. If your body is healthy and energy flows freely to and through you, then it will be possible to welcome opportunities to expand your career and draw financial energy into your life.

Conversely, if you are run-down, exhausted, or tense, energy in your body is out of balance and depleted. Opportunities to welcome energy in the form of earnings may present themselves, but your personal energy will not be sufficient to maintain the flow of abundance. When this happens, you may feel overwhelmed by work demands, lack of connection to your work, and so on. You may also become prone to losing sight of gratitude for the opportunities surrounding you. If left unchecked, this imbalance or energy depletion can result in your body demanding intervention. Your body may become sick or prone to injury. Your Higher Consciousness (Spirit/Higher Self) may also intervene and turn down the flow of opportunities, recognizing that you are not able to manage all that is on your plate. Unfortunately, this may lead you to try to run faster on the hamster wheel of work to generate more abundance while unintentionally placing more strain on your physical body and depleting yourself of even more energy.

This exercise is great to do on a regular basis as an ounce of prevention, but it is especially important if you feel like you are on a hamster wheel of working harder and not getting anywhere.

Queen of Pentacles Grounding Exercise

♛ Find a quiet, private space, preferably though not necessarily outdoors. It is also preferable that you stand for this exercise if possible. If you must sit, try to ensure that both feet are flat on the ground or floor. Allow this meditation to take anywhere from five to ten minutes.

♛ Allow your eyes to close.

♛ Take a moment to notice your breath's natural cycle.

♛ After a few regular breaths, allow your breathing to soften, slow, and deepen.

♛ Allow any thoughts or worries to fade into the background of your consciousness, bringing your awareness to your center.

♛ As you breathe and relax further, envision a beautiful, calming, healing light in the center of your being.

♛ Breathe deeper into relaxation and notice this beam of light extend down through your body, through your legs, to the bottoms of your feet.

♛ Notice the color of this light and how it feels running through your body and into the Earth, easily and naturally.

♛ As you continue to breathe, allow each exhalation release excess or unneeded tension, stress, or nervous energy.

- ♛ Imagine this beam of light flowing beneath the Earth and become a root system. This root system plants you into the Earth, holds you securely, and nourishes you.

- ♛ Feel the energy rise up from the Earth through this beam of light, a healing, cleansing, strengthening root system.

- ♛ Notice it flow up through your body, eventually reaching the top of your head. Allow this to happen at the pace the energy comes to you; there is no need to rush or think about it, simply allow the energy to flow and fill you.

- ♛ When you feel grounded and rooted, imagine you are seeing your reflection in a mirror, and when you see yourself, you are the Queen of Pentacles. See the aspect of yourself that is naturally strong, healthy, abundant, robust yet also grounded, calm, and centered. This reflection may look like you or be completely different. Allow what arises to be correct for you now.

- ♛ When you are ready, you may gently open your eyes and return to your day grounded and refreshed.

Gratitude for Releasing Money

This week, practice gratitude for paying your bills. Why? If you are paying a bill, it means the following:

- ♛ You are clearing energetic (money) imbalances and creating harmony by exchanging energy (money) for energy (a product or service).

- ♛ You are receiving something (a utility, home, car, etc.), and this is a blessing.

- ♛ You are generating money (energy), which can be used to pay the bill in the first place.

- ♛ You are releasing money (energy) into the world so that abundance can continue to circulate.

- ♛ When you are writing a check or making a payment, send out a prayer of thanks and acknowledge the blessing of paying bills.

Week 15

Watch Your Language!

This week keep a list in your journal of words or phrases you commonly use to describe yourself. Think of how you introduce yourself to others. What words do you use to explain who you are and what you value?

Are these words in alignment with your ideal self and your future life vision? If not, what words would you like to use to describe yourself—even if you don't think they are true yet?

Pay attention to language as it paves the path for how we treat others and how others treat us. Are there certain phrases you need to eliminate from your life? In what ways do you want others to see/describe you?

This week begin talking to and about yourself using the words you want to be associated with.

Week 16

Practicing Patience

This week, connect with your Inner Queen of Pentacles for the power of stability, patience, and abundance. Great results take time and consistency. Before starting your daily activities, practice saying this mantra out loud every day this week.

"Thank you Spirit (or deity name) for creating the opportunities for me to manifest (goal)."

Trust that the stage is being set for you to take the next steps, and be ready to take action when opportunities arise.

WEEK 17

REVISITING YOUR COMMITMENTS

How are you doing on your commitments? Is it time to invite new commitments and actions into your routines?

Connect with your Inner Queen of Swords to help you discern what commitments require renewed energy, which can be released, as well as what new commitments will aid in creating the life you desire.

WEEK 18

ANGER ALCHEMY

Conflicts stem from differing appraisals of a situation. The more you feel like your livelihood, self, security, or status is threatened by a conflict, the angrier your reaction will be.

Anger can be a powerful catalyst if used wisely. This week let your anger be an alarm, alerting you to a perceived injustice or threat. Before reacting on impulse, however, take the time to explore if the threat is genuine or perceived.

Is the other person intentionally working to destroy you? Or are they trying to get their own needs met and perhaps not realizing the impact of their words or actions?

What purpose is your anger serving?

What actions could help you resolve the conflict? Is there something you need to say but are afraid to express? Is there a part of the conflict you can change or control—in yourself not for the other person?

There is a formula for using anger as a catalyst to build bridges rather than burning them . . .

When you are in a reasonably calm state of mind—calm enough to both express yourself and allow the other person to express him- or herself—follow this formula:

"I felt (emotion; use the list below to help clarify if needed) when you (behavior), and I would feel (desired emotion) if you (desired action)."

Angry, annoyed, agitated, afraid, alarmed, demeaned, controlled, unimportant, abandoned, forgotten, alienated, jealous, insecure, undermined, confused, manipulated, lost, hurt, disgusted, disappointed, depressed, hopeless, irritated, slighted, ignored, insulted, guilty, ashamed, embarrassed, inferior, doubtful, humiliated, lonely, isolated, singled out, scapegoated, disrespected, vulnerable, concerned, anxious, worried, sad, desperate.

Example:

If someone arriving late to a meeting triggers anger because you feel disrespected, your statement may go like this:

"I felt disrespected when you came to the meeting late. I would feel happy if you arrived on time in the future."

The essential and often overlooked step in this process is to be sure to allow the other person to express how they felt as well, without judging or invalidating their perceptions. This takes practice, so take your time and try it out when you are in conflict this week—and in the future!

WEEK 19

IF I WEREN'T AFRAID

Studies of those in hospice care reveal that one of the regrets most often expressed by the dying is of having been held back from experiencing a full life because of fear. Fear of what others would think, fear of what would happen if . . . , fear of losing someone's approval.

How would you live, talk, act, if you weren't afraid of the judgment of others? What if you weren't afraid of failure?

What would you give yourself permission to do if fear were not in your way?

Journal on these questions today and spend this week practicing moving beyond the fears that keep you from embracing the future ideal life you desire.

WEEK 20

LOVE CHALLENGE

Spend today expressing your love, appreciation, thanks, and compassion to as many people, situations, and entities (yes, Spirit Guides and Spirit Beings connect with us when we express love as well!) as you can.

Be sure to include yourself in this practice!

Align with your Inner Queen of Cups through meditation. See yourself becoming her, or sit in quiet meditation and invite the Inner Queen of Cups energy within you to come forward. As you feel, see, or sense this aspect of yourself emerging, what do you notice? Ask your Inner Queen of Cups how you can be more receptive to love and be more unconditionally loving in return.

Be open to what she offers as guidance in the form of words, visions, images, colors, symbols, scenes, memories, or perceptions that arise in your mind or body.

Express love and gratitude for the many aspects of yourself including your vulnerability and ability to give and receive love.

This week practice being open to sharing and receiving love with others.

Week 21

Follow the (Inner) Leader

List the traits you admire in a strong leader or courageous role model. List people in your life, history, or even favorite stories who exemplify strength and leadership.

How do you see yourself as a leader?

A leader doesn't have to be a CEO, president, or commander. A leader can be one who sets the trends, shows by example, and rallies others to a cause. A leader can be one who inspires others.

Set an intention every day this week to follow the guidance of your Inner Leader. Let the Queen of Wands guide you as a leader in ideas, the Queen of Swords as a leader in actions, the Queen of Cups as a leader in the home or in relationships, and the Queen of Pentacles as a financial or business leader.

Week 22

Nurturing vs. Codependency

Maternal energy facilitates life and growth. You may be a mother to children, a caregiver for a loved one or a dog, or even a nurturer of ideas. Nurturing from a place of unconditional love promotes openness, acceptance, and mutually fulfilling relationships. This requires trust not only in others but in ourselves. Often we begin nurturing from unconditional love, yet become susceptible to our own insecurities and fear-based blocks. When this happens, we subconsciously and unintentionally replace nurturing with controlling behavior, or we believe we are acting out of love or self-sacrifice when truly we are acting out of fear of abandonment or attempts to control others. Use the exercise below to clear your energy of the fears and blocks that create codependent energy in your relationships. By clearing these insecurities, you will be opening up to nurturing and loving unconditionally.

- ♛ Find a quiet private space for this meditation. Sit or lie down with eyes closed, preferably with legs and arms uncrossed.

- ♛ Take a few calming breaths and notice how your breathing becomes slower and more relaxed.

- ♛ Set the intention that you will be aligning with your Inner Queen of Cups to heal fears and insecurities in your relationships.

- ♛ As you continue to breathe and allow yourself to relax deeper, invite your Queen of Cups within to join you in this healing.

- ♛ Take a moment to notice what emerges naturally for you. Remember you may perceive the presence of this energy through any or all of your senses.

- ♛ When you are ready, and knowing you are safe and protected in this process, invite the Queen of Cups to share her mirror with you. In this mirror, you can see your fears, insecurities, and blocks reflected back to you. Allow your Inner Queen of Cups to be your tour guide, leading you through scenes that bring to your awareness the power you have given to fears and insecurities.

- ♛ Remembering to breathe and relax throughout this process, allowing any emotion that may need to be released to flow through you.

- ♛ Now imagine that you are presented with a chalice. See the colors or symbols or shape of this chalice and yourself holding the chalice with both hands. Hold the chalice before your Heart chakra in the center of your chest.

- ♛ Ask for the strength and guidance of your Inner Queen of Cups to allow you to open your heart and release any stagnant or self-sabotaging energy, any resentments, doubts, or pain.

- ♛ Sense the energy shifting in your Heart chakra. Perhaps you sense it as a change in temperature or feel movement; you may hear sounds or experience a flow as if energy is rushing from your Heart chakra like water. See or sense the energy you release as it pours into the chalice before you.

👑 When you are ready, return the chalice now filled with energy you have released to the Queen of Cups, entrusting her with this energy, which she will neutralize and release back to the Universe.

👑 Once again the Queen of Cups presents you with the mirror, only this time, your mirror is clear and reflects back to you pure, unconditional love. See yourself in this mirror experiencing pure joy, love, healing, and being completely fulfilled in life and in relationships. See yourself able to trust yourself and others. See yourself happy and accepting of others.

👑 As you see the scenes and images of deep, pure, unconditional love being reflected back to you in the mirror, you are reminded that the love you share returns to you. As you see this reflected in the mirror, you also feel your Heart chakra once again being filled with loving, healing energy.

👑 Bring your awareness to your Heart chakra, and notice how it feels as it is once again filled with and immersed in the healing, loving energy of acceptance and joy, positive regard for others and for yourself. Allow it to fill to overflowing, and expanding to share this love energy with those around you.

👑 Thank your Inner Queen of Cups for her healing and love, and allow her to return to her place within your energy.

👑 When you are ready, take three long relaxing breaths, and allow your eyes to open.

Drink plenty of water throughout the day as you have shifted energy through this exercise and water will continue the healing, clearing process. Throughout the rest of the week, be mindful of your expressions of love and nurturing toward others. With a clean slate it will now be easier for you to discern if your actions stem from unconditional love or fear and control. When you need help discerning between the two, ask for the guidance of your Inner Queen of Cups.

WEEK 23

GIVING

How can you give of yourself this week? Clean house! Let go, donate, release both physical items and emotional energy. Invest in releasing with the intention of sharing abundance with others and/or creating space for growth for yourself every day this week.

Consider using a quantitative goal to stay motivated (a little Queen of Swords energy kicking in here . . .) such as releasing five physical items each day. Envision that you are clearing space to help generate the flow of abundance. For example by donating an old chair, envision what purpose you want that corner of the room, now vacant, to serve. Will that be the future home of a new chair or a plant? By giving a gift of your old bicycle or a bag of clothes you no longer wear, what new energy can you invite into your home or life that better aligns with your current goals?

It may help to make a list of what you would like to attract into your life first and then see yourself creating space for this new abundance by sharing your current wealth with others and releasing what is no longer needed.

WEEK 24

HERITAGE

Spend a moment reflecting on the ancestors you never met—those who passed before your great-great-grandparents were born. You don't even need to know their names.

Imagine a conversation with them. Invite them to share what their dreams were for you.

Journal a conversation or letter from your ancestors to your present self. To help connect with the energy of your ancestors and give thanks for their sacrifices, consider offering blessings, a prayer, or other tokens (stones, flowers, poems, etc.) in a designated space in your home on a table or an altar dedicated to honoring family and ancestors. You may decorate this space with photos or other reminders of your ancestral heritage. Also, you may draw on their wisdom and strength through conversations with them like the one in this exercise. Don't worry about whether you feel you are making it up. Whether you believe in spirit communication or simply in the power of the subconscious mind, remember you are engaging a part of yourself connected to your ancestors.

Now write a letter to your future generations, describing the foundation you are creating and the sacrifice you are making as a gift to them. Imagine the positive impact your life and legacy are creating for generations to come.

Draw, write, or create a visual representation of this large-scale legacy. Use this to motivate you to reach your goals.

WEEK 25

FINE-TUNE YOUR INTUITION

Practice trusting your intuition. At least one time each day this week, quiet your mind through focus on your breathing. Ask your Higher Self or Spirit for guidance on a question or issue, and then await the answer. You may use the Inner Queen Intuitive Log to note the outcome of your intuitive practice sessions.

Practice this first in small ways—in benign choices prior to checking the internet or asking expert advice. Then follow up with your external search and note whether the answers that come from the outside world match the answers you receive from within.

Note the following:

How do your guides most frequently communicate with you? What blocks, fears, or doubts emerge in your practice? Ask your guides for help in moving beyond these barriers. The Queen of Cups, for instance, can help you go with the flow; the Queen of Swords can help cut through blocks; etc.

What differences in energy or perception do you notice when information turns out to be more accurate vs. less accurate? It is worth tracking both successes and inaccuracies because this will help you discern between the perception of intuitive information as opposed to the perception of information stemming from ego desires or fears.

Week 26

Intuitive Eating

This week's exercise works with the energy of the Queen of Pentacles and the earthy energy of nutrition, the physical body, and health.

Before selecting the food or beverages that will nurture your body, pause to intuitively reflect on whether your food choices are in alignment with what your body needs in a given moment. Before reaching for the most convenient snack, food, or grocery item, take a little time to center yourself and ask if the food you feel drawn to is serving your highest nutritional energy needs.

This is not a commitment to a diet, it is a process of selecting nutrients based on what your body's wisdom is guiding you toward and avoiding foods your body is not served by eating on a moment-to-moment basis. Use the meditation below to help you get started.

Listening to the Body with the Queen of Pentacles

- ♛ Find a comfortable, private space for this meditation. Allow your eyes to close and take a few moments to quiet your mind by becoming aware of your breathing process.

- ♛ After a few relaxing breaths, invite your Inner Queen of Pentacles to join you and help you listen to your body.

- ♛ You may perceive her presence visually, in your mind's eye; however, for this exercise it is just as beneficial to tune in to the physical sensations of your body. Practice feeling her presence.

- ♛ Take note of the various sensations in your body, free from judgment or the need to change anything in this moment.

- ♛ Allow yourself to settle into your body with every breath, becoming more aware of your physical energy and the various sensations.

- If you experience any discomfort in your body, allow yourself to breathe, relax, and notice if you then experience energetic shifts releasing the discomfort.
- You may also tune in to the discomfort and ask what it is trying to show you or what it needs in order to heal.
- When you are ready, feel, see, sense yourself becoming so closely attuned to your body that you can feel, hear, or see it communicating with you. Notice how your body is communicating with you.
- Set an intention that you are listening deeply to your body and that you will continue to listen to and honor your body throughout this day and the days ahead.
- When you are ready, thank your Inner Queen of Pentacles for her guidance and wisdom, and return from this meditation.

Now as you continue your day and in the days ahead, pause to connect to your body at various times, especially when making decisions about nutrition and food. Before selecting different foods ask your body, "Do you need this?" Listen to your body's signals of thirst, hunger, or exhaustion, and honor your body's requests.

There are no permanent restrictions to follow. This is a process of letting the sensations in your body guide you to what you need most at a given time.

Try this for a week and notice any differences in how you feel. You can always choose to adapt this technique on an ongoing basis once you experience the results of listening to your body's wisdom.

WEEK 27

DRAWING ON YOUR VISION

Visualize the life you are creating. Then take your meditative practice a step further: Draw, collage, or otherwise create a visual image or representation of the life you desire.

You can always change your mind, but for now this image is a focal point that draws on the energy needed to manifest. Art was one of the original tools of working Magick in ancient times, so you are calling in the vision you have in your mind and giving it a physical form. This allows for manifestation to begin to take place. Set aside any doubts or worries about not being an artist. You have creative energy as a woman. Whether you choose to draw or make a collage, you are using your creativity to craft a focal point for manifestation energy.

Remember, the power of intention guides your energy. Prior to embarking on this exercise, consciously invite the Queen of Wands to assist you in creating your intention and giving it a visual form.

WEEK 28

ASK FOR HELP

The beautiful thing about living in a world with eight billion other people (and counting) is that it does not fall on any of us individually to have all of the answers. Seek guidance from within, and balance this with a willingness to receive guidance from the outside as well.

Set an intention this week that you are ready to receive guidance from teachers and helpers on your path.

Some of your teachers may be obvious—mentors, coaches, experts, and consultants. Others may be subtler—adversaries, random strangers, peers, neighbors, friends, family. . . . This week be open to the lessons all can impart to you in ordinary moments.

This week, journal your experiences asking for help and accepting input from others.

WEEK 29

DETOX TIME!

The Inner Queen of Swords is an ace at helping you find your passion, confidence, and focus.

Draw on her energy this week to help you align your focus by cutting out distractions.

The Inner Queen of Swords will help you sharpen your focus, but like the sharp edge of the sword, your keen instincts are leading you to take action that may seem edgy to some.

Use the energy of this cutting edge to pare down activities that drain your energy. TV, social media, excess worry, perfectionistic behaviors, gossiping, negative thinking, complaining . . . these are just some examples of behaviors and thought patterns that can weigh you down over time. Take the sword to some of these activities, or others that you notice drain you of energy or time.

Using a timer, become self-aware of mental chatter, and notice what household or work routines are redundant and no longer serving you.

Give yourself a seven-day detox from the three biggest things that distract you from your goals.

WEEK 30

SAYING NO HELPS YOU SAY YES

Use the energy of the Inner Queen of Swords to cut out what is not serving the highest good this week. Following your week of detox from distractions, this week draw on the strength of your Inner Queen of Swords to help you set boundaries. By setting limits with others you are freeing yourself from obligations that help you sabotage your growth. Use your connection to this Queen to discern which situations or obligations truly need your energy and to what extent. For example, rather than going to the extreme of creating such high walls around yourself that you cut off all connection to others in the name of setting boundaries, get in the healthy habit of checking in with the Inner Queen of Swords on a case by case basis. Ask if certain activities, commitments, or obligations are truly serving the highest good for all at this time, and trust this intuitive guidance to help you set limits where appropriate.

Notice that the highest good is not always what you want the most. Use boundaries in the service of the highest good for all involved this week. This may involve saying no to people who ask for what is not in your best interest to give or in their best interest to receive.

Saying no for the highest good allows you to heal and allows others to find resources within themselves that may have gone untapped. Also, by saying no, you are also allowing space in your life to say yes to new experiences.

WEEK 31

THE POWER OF MOTHER NATURE

Bring some plants into your home or workspace. If you are still working on your green thumb, consider an already started plant as opposed to seeds. Talk to your plant, name her, sing to her, feel her energy when you feed her and interact with her.

Share loving, kind thoughts and words with your plant and notice what happens!

While you are bringing the wilderness indoors, don't forget to commune with the greater wilderness outdoors as well. Spend some time each day in nature even if it is a short walk on your lunch break.

Give yourself five minutes among plants or trees in their natural environment without the distractions of conversation or music. Can you sense the energy of the wilderness around you?

Do this for a week and journal the differences you notice in your feelings, thoughts, sensations, intuition and overall wellness.

WEEK 32

HEALING AND CLEARING

Turn your natural daily routines of cleansing the body into energy-cleansing activities. It is as simple as setting intentions.

Prior to washing your hands, showering, or brushing your teeth, set a mental intention that you are removing and releasing all energies unintentionally carried from day-to-day experiences. Set an intention that in doing so you are realigning your body's natural energy flow for optimum circulation of healthy, clear energy.

You may also choose to visualize different color energy fields—also known as auras, which are there even if you can't see them. As you shower or wash, imagine the purest, brightest color energy filling your aura. Imagine or visualize yourself clearing murky or muddy-colored energy from your body's aura. Imagine that your cleansing process is creating a healthy, pure, vibrant, light or bright aura.

Week 33

Deep Listening

Set an intention at the beginning of each day this week that in every conversation you will focus first on listening.

Make this an enjoyable game, as if you are listening deeply for clues to really understand and know the person speaking to you.

Imagine that you have all the time in the world to make your point and be fully understood, and the most interesting and exciting thing is to know another person deeply.

Practice this for each day this week. What do you notice?

Week 34

Connecting to Abundance

Take some time to reflect on abundance energy this week.

What is your long-term vision of abundance? Be specific. If you want to earn $70,000 per year, and have a car, house, and a set number of dollars in assets or a business worth $100,000, list the concrete items in terms of specific assets.

For each item on your list, write down the purpose served by this item—for example, a five-bedroom house serves the goal of secure living quarters for your family and a home office.

For each item, write down the steps you need to take to get closer to your goal.

Now look at your actual records of financial resources—savings statements, net worth statements, etc.

The goal is not to feel the gap between what you have and what you want, but rather to take an honest appraisal of where you are and where you want to be.

Make a list of actions you could undertake to get from where you are to where you want to be financially.

Use the Inner Queen of Pentacles energy of abundance to invite opportunities to bridge the gap between where you are and where you would like to be. Practice envisioning and perceiving your connection to the energy of the Inner Queen of Pentacles. In the process remember to express gratitude for the starting point and all of the small steps bringing you to your goal.

WEEK 35

ANCESTRAL HEALING

It has long been understood that traumas and wounds can be multi-generational. In other words, the impact of addiction, illness, abuse, and personal or cultural traumas affect not only individuals, but also entire families. Even the great-grandchildren of survivors of war, famine, or oppression feel the attitudes, fears, beliefs, and emotions modeled through the generations. Add to this new breakthrough discoveries that trauma and oppression can be passed down genetically, and it becomes clear that in addition to living our own lives, we are also living with the impact of those who lived before us.

For example, a young person of color in modern-day America may not have had a personal experience of slavery or overt government-enforced segregation, but the collective experience of her family and community brings this into her life. The trauma, grief, and feelings of her ancestors live as part of her heritage alongside many positive attributes. The injustices our ancestors experienced linger in our consciousness and in society. Another example is the impact of economic devastation. A grandchild of a survivor of the Great Depression may not know firsthand the level of desperation her grandparents experienced, but her attitudes toward money, her feelings of economic security or lack thereof, and her relationship with food may all be influenced by the attitudes and experiences of her predecessors. Likewise, a woman whose mother was a victim of incest may have been spared the trauma in her own upbringing, but nevertheless her relationships with others, views on sexuality, and perhaps even body image may be shaped by her mother's experience as her mother is one of her primary role models. Children and grandchildren of people with addictions or victims of domestic violence also carry the wounds created generations ago, either through a vulnerability to continue the cycle of addiction or abuse or by structuring life to avoid certain triggers. This is not a matter of blame or shaming our parents and grandparents but simply a realization that we inherit a lot more than eye and hair color. We also inherit the collective experiences, joys, sorrows, opportunities, and oppressions of our ancestors. But just as cycles of domestic violence, addiction, and discrimination can be broken, so too, can we work to heal inherited wounds both within the family and the larger society.

This week work with the Queens of Pentacles and Cups to explore multigenerational wounds and patterns from your family. You may make a list of strengths, skills, specialties, and positive experiences passed down from your family as well as a list of patterns of wounds, losses, oppression, traumas, and cycles of violence or illness/addictions. Practice this exercise with reverence for your ancestors, recognizing their contributions in light of their challenges.

👑 With the help of your Higher Self and Spirit Guides, call on the Queen of Pentacles to connect you to the Earth and securely anchor you in the present moment. See the Queen of Pentacles before you, and feel her energy merge with your own until you see yourself strong, solid, and rooted to the Earth.

👑 Next call on the Queen of Cups. Again, visualize her in front of you, and feel her presence as comforting, healing, and ready to help you release and heal. Allow her to embrace you, sense her energy merge with your own, and see yourself embodying her strengths.

👑 Next, ask for the help of your guides and ancestors in the spirit world. Ask for the assistance of those who are ready to bring healing. Be open to all of your senses as you may see, hear, feel, smell, or perceive their presence in any number of ways.

👑 Ask for a symbol of what it is you would like to heal from your lineage. Allow your guides to show you again through all or any of your senses.

👑 Ask for their help in releasing the wounds from your ancestors. Notice how your guides help you to release this energy.

👑 When you feel the energy move through you and understand your session is complete, thank all who have helped you in this working.

Allow for plenty of rest and water after this exercise as you have shifted a lot of energy.

Week 36

Manifestation Tree

Refer back to your original big vision goal from earlier this year. What clarification have you received? Connect to your intuition, and ask your Spirit Guides to show you the next step on the ladder to manifesting your big vision. Use the following meditation to connect fully to the energy of manifestation. Think of this exercise as giving roots and branches to your goal—anchoring you to the ground, giving you the patience and energetic nourishment you need to remain stable as your dream manifests, while also allowing you to stretch beyond your comfort zone and expand in the direction of your goals.

Manifestation Tree Meditation

Begin with the next stage in your advancement toward your goal. If you have several conflicting goals or several desires at once, sit with your guides to clarify which of these goals most needs your attention.

- ♛ Find a private, quiet space to do this meditation exercise. Get into a comfortable position and allow your eyes to close.

- ♛ Take three slow, comfortable breaths to settle your energy. Set the intention that you are relaxing and releasing any distractions.

- ♛ When you are ready, invite your Inner Queen of Pentacles to join you, and ask her to help you cultivate strength and patience and to ground you to the Earth. Add any other requests for connection with her unique strengths. Allow a few moments to feel, sense, see, hear, or perceive the presence of the Queen of Pentacles within and around you.

- ♛ As you continue to breathe and relax, imagine a powerful, healing, energetic light beginning in the center of your being, descending downward through your body, and moving out the soles of your feet into the Earth. See the color of this column of light. Feel its warmth, and notice any other sensations accompanying this sturdy column of light.

- ♛ Imagine any distractions, obstacles, or blockages that you are free to release, being flushed out through this column of light. See, feel, or perceive these obstacles being completely released, and easily, effortlessly flowing down through this column of light into the center of the Earth where they will be recycled.

- ♛ Feel the shift within your body, mind, and spirit as these energy blocks are released.

- ♛ When you are ready, notice with every inhalation that you are drawing healing, nurturing, strong light from the Earth, up through the soles of your feet, up your legs, and back into the core of your being. Notice the color, sensation, and appearance of this light. Notice how your body feels as you receive this healing light energy.

- ♛ Once you feel the energy flowing easily and effortlessly through your core, notice it overflowing and rising up your body to the top of your head. This beautiful healing energy reaches your Crown chakra and spills out in all directions.

- ♛ Experience the sensations you feel, sense, see, or hear as this circuit of light energy fills your being.

- ♛ When you are ready, bring an image of your desired goal, your intention for this exercise, into your mind. Imagine your goal accomplished successfully portrayed before your eyes as a scene or picture of success.

- ♛ Let your breath slow and deepen further into relaxation and see the scene of your future success being drawn into your body. Feel the sensations of your goal merging with your body and becoming part of you.

- ♛ Now draw your awareness to the center of your being and feel, sense, or see a bright, brilliant ball of light, fueled by the image of your success, your goal accomplished. See, feel, and perceive this energy ball extending first down your legs, then out through the soles of your feet, and into the ground.

Imagine this energy creating your root system, anchoring you to the ground.

👑 As you breathe and relax, imagine, sense, and feel powerful, loving, nurturing energy coming from deep within the Earth and feeding your root system. Imagine your roots drinking up this nurturing, healing, empowering energy and bringing it up through your body.

👑 Continue to breathe as this energy expands, strengthens, and grows, traveling up through your body and out of the top of your head, passing through your Crown chakra.

👑 See this energy flowing from your roots to the top of your head and beyond as expanding and creating branches—an energy matrix that will expand, grow, and stretch, bringing you past any restrictions, beyond limitations, and into your best potential future.

👑 See, sense, and feel these branches carrying this powerful, nurturing energy from the Earth, through your body, feeding your goal, and bringing it to fruition. These branches carry your intention out into the universe where it is manifesting.

👑 Trust that this goal has already been energetically manifested and you are the tree, spreading and growing in all directions.

👑 Trust that your goal continues to derive nurturing and strength from the Earth and that your goal has deep roots, a strong trunk, and flexible branches, that you continue to feed energy into this goal, and it strengthens as well.

👑 When you are ready, thank your Inner Queen of Pentacles, and trust that she is continuing to work with you. Allow your eyes to open.

Repeat this visualization periodically to strengthen your focus and help you feel secure and grounded on your path. Remember to ask for clarification from your guides before choosing an intention to strengthen with this meditation, to ensure you are working collaboratively with your Higher Self for your best potential outcome.

WEEK 37

MONEY AND VALUE

Money can trigger strong emotional reactions: insecurity, fear, craving, self-doubt, resentment, joy, jealousy. Remember that money is a tangible way to measure energy exchange. When we assign value to money, we are finding a convenient means to show how much time, effort, energy, work is worth the exchange for a resource in the form of a material item, clothing, food, or an experience such as a movie or vacation.

Make a list of your core values and reflect on the ways you carry these values on your path. Next, make a list of any fears, doubts, worries, or negative beliefs you have about money.

Once you have clarified both lists, explore how you can align your values with the ways you make and invest money. How can money become a vehicle for you to express your values through the way you live? Likewise, how can a lifestyle based on your values help you receive the money you need to reinvest this energy on future resources and experiences and create the security and experiences you value?

For example, let's say your list of values includes things like generosity, charity, helping those in need, protecting the environment, and supporting child literacy, yet you notice that your attitudes and beliefs about money contain items such as "money makes people greedy," "people fight over money," "I feel secure when I have money," or "I feel guilty if I have more money than someone else in need."

You could explore ways to reconcile what at first seems to be a discrepancy between your values and attitudes toward money. For example, by recognizing that money can be a source of security as well as a vehicle that allows you to contribute to your favorite charities and helps you support child literacy programs, you could construct an empowered, effective budget and financial plan drawing on your motivation to be generous and charitable, while investing enough in yourself first to create a sustainable cash flow. By encompassing your concern for charity, you are diminishing the likelihood of getting entangled in the temptation to become greedy or susceptible to the behaviors associated with the negative connotations held about money.

Make your Values List and your Money Beliefs/Attitudes List and then work on your own plan to integrate the two, creating a strategy for accepting financial abundance as a means of generating future experiences that add value to your life.

WEEK 38

THINK GLOBALLY–
QUEENING UP THE WORLD

If you could be a catalyst for one significant change in society, what would it be?

What would society look like if your cause were successful? Why is this cause important to you?

How is your current work helping to bring this change into society?

What can you do on a daily basis to be a part of this solution in a positive way?

How does this change relate to your ultimate goal and your ideal future self?

WEEK 39

WORKING WITH WILLPOWER

Free will holds a special place in the shared consciousness of many cultures today. Willpower, free will, and individuality correspond to the energy of the Queen of Swords. It is little wonder that we place such an emphasis on the warrior aspect of ourselves. As women, we have fought hard to assert ourselves in a patriarchal society. As strides have been made to fight for equality—also a specialty of the Queen of Swords—many women have attuned themselves to the patriarchal concept of power in the form of dominance, aggression, or aligning with masculine energy.

It is as if culturally, we have deposed the archetypes of the mother as the Queen of Cups and of nature as the Queen of Pentacles, in favor of the strength of wit in the Queen of Wands and the willpower of the Queen of Swords. We must remember that no one archetypal power supersedes the other three. Each represents power, yet they are powers of various kinds.

This point is crucial to understanding the delicate balance of exerting free will while remaining receptive to the flow of opportunities. In other words, we need to find the equilibrium between remaining dedicated to our values and commitments and not getting lost in power struggles stemming from the desires of the ego. It is keeping the big picture, some of which we may not be able to see clearly, in harmony with the immediate, which may seem easier to control or more obvious to understand.

Thus, we must periodically reflect, especially when perceiving blockages or struggles in our midst, upon whether it is the will of our Ego Self or Higher Self that we are serving through our actions. When our perception of power is challenged, when it seems like life has become an uphill battle, when we become exhausted by our efforts to create change, feeling that doors are not opening fast enough, or we are not getting the cooperation or opportunities we feel we deserve, where is this coming from? There are differences between our desires, our will, and our higher good. The more we can work on blending the energy of projecting our intentions with the practice of being receptive to collaborating with our guides, the more balanced, and ultimately better off, we will be.

Take a moment to list your current goals and intentions. What practices, thoughts, attitudes, or goals are consuming most of your energy at this point? Thoughts can consume energy by taking up mental space in the form of obsessions, ruminations, or preoccupation with events, ideas, or desires.

Now review your list. Let your intuition guide you to one of your listed items that needs attention right now. Sit for a moment with this issue in your mind. Invite your Inner Queen of Swords to join you. Ask her if this issue is adding energy to your life or taking energy from it. Ask her if this goal is creating power struggles, serving your ego, or your Higher Self. If you feel stuck or confused, take a few deep breaths and allow yourself to center. You may also wish to invite your Inner Queen of Cups to balance this meditation, asking for help harmonizing the drive to manifest with the intuition to receive guidance for the best possible outcome.

WEEK 40

ACCEPTING LOSS

Make peace with loss. What has been removed from your path, your past, or your life is in service of clearing the space for creating future opportunities.

What losses do you struggle to accept?

Visualize the empty space where a loss exists as an open cup awaiting fulfillment with new blessings, love, opportunity, support, and people.

Practice this visualization whenever you are reminded of the empty space: Imagine the space is a reserved seat at a table. It is just waiting for the next person or opportunity to become a part of your journey.

Week 41

Dialing In All Four Queens

Use the following visualization to balance and harmonize the energies of all of the Four Queens this week.

- ♛ Find a private, quiet space to get comfortable.

- ♛ Allow your eyes to close and bring your awareness to your natural breathing process.

- ♛ After taking a few relaxing deep breaths, feel that, as you breathe, stress, tension, and distractions are drifting away.

- ♛ When you are ready, invite your Inner Queen of Wands to join you. Invite her to show you the level of Wands energy in your system at this time. Imagine this energy as a beam of yellow light. Before trying to fix or change it, just notice the yellow light. How big is it? What does the intensity feel like? Do you sense heat or cold from this energy?

- ♛ Once you have taken a few moments to perceive the level of your Inner Queen of Wands energy, allow your breath to calm and relax deeper. Set the intention that you are consciously resetting your Inner Queen of Wands energy to a balanced, harmonious baseline that is appropriate for you. For example, if your Queen of Wands energy is too intense, you may envision it dropping and leveling off. If it feels insufficient or distant, you may see it become stronger or taller. Allow the energy to shift in alignment with your intention of bringing the Inner Queen of Wands energy into the ideal state of balance and harmony that is appropriate for you at this time.

- ♛ When you are ready, invite your Inner Queen of Swords to present the level of your Swords energy as a visible red beam of light. Without making any changes notice the size, intensity, proximity, and perception of this energy as it is in your life right now.

- ♛ In your own time, ask for guidance in adjusting the energy to optimal functioning for your needs right now. Allow any sensations to arise as your Queen of Swords energy is adjusted to meet your current needs. Trust that your energy is being balanced and harmonized to optimal functioning.

- ♛ When you feel ready, repeat this process for the Queen of Cups as a blue light, then the Queen of Pentacles as a green light.

- ♛ Finally, thank your Inner Queens and guides for bringing your energy into balance and harmony. Allow your eyes to open.

Repeat this exercise periodically as needed.

WEEK 42

IN THE SHADOW

Give your dark side an outlet this week. Success requires a balance between the civilized, polished drives of the outer personality and the creative outlet of our wild side within.

What longings or urges are you experiencing and keeping hidden because they are not polite?

What are these urges trying to tell you about what is missing in your life?

For example, an urge to confront your boss and scream or blow up in an unprofessional way may signify that you are feeling unheard or mounting pressure that you don't have a proper work-based outlet for.

Many great writers and artists became successful by creating fantasy stories or works of art or music expressing what they would have liked to do but would not out of respect for the law, their health, or others. Let the Shadow side of yourself speak through art, collage, poetry, a letter you write but don't send, or a story this week.

What do you learn as a result of tuning in to your Shadow?

WEEK 43

THE WISDOM OF CHILDREN

Open your mind to the wisdom of young people this week. The Inner Queen of Cups brings out your nurturing maternal energy. This "mother within" is not just a source of giving to others, but also of receiving guidance and wisdom from those she is nurturing. Listen intently to what young people or children are saying this week. Resist the urge to combat youthful idealism with the realism of experience. Listen as if with new ears, as if anything was possible.

What possibilities are the young reminding you of?

WEEK 44

THE WISDOM OF ELDERS

This week open your mind to the wisdom of your elders, whether they are those a few years your senior or those whose generation paved the way for yours. What wisdom do they have to offer? Resist the urge to react as if they are out of touch. Listen intently to the words of elders in your family or community. If you are not close to elders in your family, seek out elders in your profession, in your community, or in your daily travels and listen carefully to what they have to say.

What wisdom are they imparting or reminding you of?

Week 45

Ideal Future Revisited

Without referring to your ideal future vision from the beginning of this process, create a future vision of your ideal life/ideal future self based on your current values and priorities.

Now review your ideal future self/lifestyle from the beginning of this process.

What has changed?

How are you closer to your goal now than you were before?

What aspects of your ideal future have you decided no longer interest you?

Set three to five new specific, attainable, measurable goals. These may be continuations or revisions of your original goals from earlier this year. For each goal, make a list of actions to be completed in the next three months. For each goal make a list of actions to be completed in the next six months.

Week 46

Schedule for Success

Set dates on your calendar to complete each of the action steps outlined last week.

Express gratitude for the outcome of your journey so far including any changes you have made, any losses that have cleared the way for new growth, and for the abundance you have received so far. Make offerings as an expression of gratitude each day this week for the accomplishments you have made. Offerings can be prayers, blessings, food, burning incense, lighting a candle, or other expressions of gratitude to the natural and spiritual worlds.

Week 47

Where Am I Now?

Reflect on your current lifestyle. What elements of your life bring you the greatest happiness and joy?

Which aspects of your current lifestyle bring you the greatest challenges?

Which aspects of your life make you feel drained or stressed out?

If you were to successfully reach your top goals, how essential are each of the lifestyle factors that bring you stress or unpleasant feelings?

What could be different?

Ask for guidance in finding solutions to satisfy your needs without draining your energy.

Week 48

Empower Your Friendships

Make time for social connections this week. Social time is not idle; it is a valuable opportunity to share and contribute to the life of others and to receive their support and guidance.

Think of social time as an investment in your support network, which is priceless. It is also an investment in balancing your energy and in your optimal wellness.

Set a plan to make social connections and have at least one face-to-face social call this week.

WEEK 49

HEALTHY EMPATHY

We can become so emotionally connected to those around us that we absorb their energy, moods, and feelings. This is what is meant by the term *empath*. People describe being an empath as if it were a unique subculture; however, we are all empaths in that we are equipped with the ability to feel for others. Some are more sensitive to the emotional states of others and have greater difficulty letting go of another's troubles. Others react to this sensitivity by shutting down or avoiding people so as not to be bombarded with unpleasant feelings.

Notice how your mood, feelings, or energy change around various other people. Before being quick to judge the other person as the problem (they are not "bad" or "toxic"; they are simply having their own struggles), consider ways you can detach from the energy of others so that you are not carrying their emotional burdens.

Try the following:

Practice visualizing a protective bubble or shield around yourself to keep your energy in and create a barrier between the high vibrational energy you are cultivating through your daily spiritual practice and the lower vibrational energy associated with stressful situations, dense, heavy emotions, and challenges. It is the energetic pollution from daily life, not specific people per se, that is being filtered out by this shield you are creating. Intend that high-vibration energy can enter the bubble. This is the equivalent of setting an energetic security system allowing the energy that will uplift, nurture, and expand your growth, while barring the energy of stressful situations or heavy emotional states from getting in.

Use the intentional cleansing exercises practiced earlier in the year. Wash your hands and body with the intention of releasing any energy you may have been carrying that is not yours or does not serve your highest growth.

Remind yourself that other people's struggles are their gifts from the Universe. If you were to take away the pain others experience, you would also be taking away the gifts of overcoming, evolving, and growing. Call on your Inner Queen of Cups to help you experience compassion without feeling the need to solve, fix, or absorb the problems others are experiencing.

WEEK 50

CLEANSİNG CURRENT

This week we work with an energetic cleansing meditation in alliance with our Inner Queen of Cups. Practice this meditation daily and take note of differences in your emotional state, energy level, relationships with others, and physical perceptions of pain, stress, and feeling blocked or overwhelmed. We constantly pick up energy from the atmosphere around us. Just as furniture or pictures can accumulate dust periodically, so can our aura accumulate energetic residue from daily experiences. Work stress, family crises, an argument with a friend, financial worries, even the bombardment of stimulating information from social media or television can have an impact on the energy of our aura. When our aura becomes cluttered with the residue of emotional states, information, and fragments of energy from other people or places, it can have an impact on our emotional and even physical well-being.

Therefore, it is important to periodically clear your aura and release energy that is slowing down your system. Like clearing cookies from your browser, defragging your hard drive, or getting an oil change for your car, energy clearing helps reboot your system and strengthens your personal energy. The frequency with which you should clear your energy depends on your lifestyle and life experiences. If you work in a high-stress environment such as health care where you interact frequently with people in crisis or poor health, you may benefit from doing this exercise more frequently. If you have just gone through a challenging ordeal in your personal life, this exercise will also be a beneficial reset to help you move forward. Ideally, clearing energy through some meditative practice on a daily basis is great.

But realistically, making a habit of regularly clearing your energy when you feel stress mounting in your life is just fine as well.

Cleansing Current Meditation

This meditation works with the energy of your Inner Queen of Cups, whose element is Water. Find a private, peaceful place to spend some time in this meditation.

- ♛ Allow your eyes to close and take three relaxing breaths, deepening your breathing while remaining comfortable. Allow any distracting thoughts to drift to the back of your mind, and bring your awareness to your breathing process to help you relax deeper.

- ♛ Sit with this calm, deepening relaxation for a few moments.

- ♛ When you are ready, invite the energy of the Inner Queen of Cups to join you and bring cleansing, clearing, healing energy into your body.

- ♛ Imagine a beautiful, clear, crystal stream of soothing water falling gently from high above you. This is a refreshing, comfortable current. You may perceive it as light, as soothing water, or as a current of uplifting energy. Imagine this current descends from the realm of the Divine; it is pure, healing, and filled with renewing, loving, protective energy.

- ♛ See this cascading stream of gentle water pour through the top of your head at your Crown chakra. Notice its color, shape, size. Sense the energy of this stream of healing energy as it pours gently down through your head, clearing, cleansing, soothing, rejuvenating, and healing every part of your mind, eyes, ears . . . down to your neck.

- ♛ Sense the stream of healing flow through your neck, soothing any tension, clearing your throat, streaming down through your shoulders, chest, and arms into to your hands and fingers. Notice this stream of healing energy continuing to flow from above, pouring down through your body and filling every part of you with healing love, releasing and sweeping away any tension, blocks, or stagnant energy in its current.

- ♛ Feel every part of your body including your organs, bones, muscles, and nerves bathed in this healing current. Sense this current continuing to flow to the base of your spine, through your hips, down your legs, and to the soles of your feet.

- ♛ Notice that as this current descends through your body, it takes with it any unnecessary worries, tension, strain, pain, fears; anything you no longer need washes away, out through the soles of your feet and into the Earth to be recycled.

- ♛ Imagine this as a steady stream of light, and allow it to continue to flow for as long as you need it. Notice how it feels as your energy shifts, as you find greater release and freedom from tension and stress carried away by this current, and as your body is completely filled with healing, rejuvenating, fresh, crystal clear energy in this current.

- ♛ When you are ready, envision yourself as your Inner Queen of Cups. Feel yourself sparkle and shimmer, filled with this new crystal energy, this current of soothing water now circulating all through your body and bringing healing with every breath.

- ♛ Thank your Inner Queen of Cups for assisting you with this process. When you are ready, you may open your eyes and shift your awareness to the physical space around you, ready to return to your daily routines refreshed and revitalized.

WEEK 51

GET LOST

This week spend some time getting lost. Take a walk or a drive with no plan and no agenda.

How does it feel to be spontaneous again? This spontaneity connects you with the flowing, youthful energy of the Queen of Wands, who, like air, needs to travel and expand and thrives in open spaces, free of confines and limitations of daily routines and monotony. Explore your surroundings this week. Take a different route to work. Give your GPS the day off and ask your intuition where your travels should take you.

WEEK 52

ENDINGS AND BEGINNINGS

Spend time visualizing yourself, your lifestyle, and where you have come from in the past twelve months. Make a list of new aspects of your life including new hobbies, interests, work, feelings, attitudes, friends, relationships, living space, pets, and so on. Anything that was added to your life in the last twelve months, write down on this list.

In a meditation or visualization, see yourself sharing this list of new aspects of your life with yourself twelve months ago. What would your prior self have thought of all the changes that have taken place? Which are most surprising? What does your past self say or do?

Now imagine your future self twelve months from now. This future self is showing you a new list of further changes—some unimaginable, some planned.

What is she showing you? How does it feel? What wisdom does she impart to you?

INNER QUEEN
INTUITIVE LOG

As your relationship grows with the Inner Queens, it's important to keep track of your experience. Here I have included an Inner Queen Intuitive Log you can use to track your results. Remember, Queening Up is a process, so it requires patience and rehearsal. Recording your progress helps you really see your development and empowerment. Use the format on pages 146–147 as a guide to continue to develop your intuitive connection to your Higher Self through the energy of the Inner Queens. As you develop, your Higher Self/Spirit will speak to you in many ways and in many forms, but since you have become very well acquainted with the Four Queens, use them as a springboard.

Your Higher Self/Spirit will impart wisdom for your greatest good, and any messages that seem to be centered on despair, tragedy, and fear or fame, fortune, and glory are more likely aspects of the ego and not your intuition. Practice recognizing the difference between the two.

Make it a practice to revisit these entries monthly or weekly to see what insights develop after the initial meditation session. For instance, the immediate guidance you receive may be accentuated by fun coincidences later that day or week.

These coincidences are really synchronicity—the Universe's way of communicating with you through symbols and processes.

As you now arrive at the end of this book, you have probably realized it is only the beginning. Return to this book periodically and continue to work with the energy of your Inner Queen as you grow and progress along your life path.

Date: _____

Goal: _____

[What is your intention in connecting with your Inner Queens? Think of this as what you would type into a search engine if you were browsing the internet, rather than tuning in to the energy of the Universe. For example: "I want more respect at work."]

Power I needed: _____

[What feels lacking in the present? For example: "Confidence, assertiveness"]

Queen I called on: _____

[Which Queen aligns with the results you are seeking? To continue with the above example, we can use the Queen of Swords. Take a moment to meditate on the energy of the Queen of Swords. You may do this through the following techniques:
- Visualize this Queen interacting with you. What does she do or say?
- You may imagine yourself becoming this Queen. What changes when you see yourself as this Queen? What do you do/say differently?
- You may use affirming statements you imagine this Queen would say.

Or you may feel compelled to connect with this Queen's energy in another way. Experiment!]

Perceptions: _____

[Note what you sense in your body while connecting with this energy. For example, you may sense energy vibrations, a pulse, heat, cold, light, sounds, or none of the above. Be open to the experience you have!]

Feelings: _____

[How do you feel as you connect with this Queen?]

Message/Images/symbols received: _____

[A message does not have to be verbal. It can be an image, symbol, sensation, feeling, or a sudden "knowing." You may feel as if a scene is playing out in your mind, or you may feel a sense of understanding. You may feel at first like you have made up the message. Set doubts aside. Even if you have made it up, it is inspired by your Higher Self, and any message generated by love and compassion is serving you in some way.

   In keeping with the above example, you may see an image of the Queen of Swords in your office standing behind your chair holding out a lantern to you.]

To me this means: _____

[Now you interpret the perceptions, images, symbols, and message based on your own association. For example, if I associate the lantern with guidance and truth, then the message from the above is that the energy I need to be assertive will be with me at work, and that even if it is difficult, I will be bringing truth to others.]

End result: _____

[What was different as a result of connecting with this Queen? For example, did you speak or act differently at work, or feel more confident, etc.?]

Date: _____

Goal: _____
_____
_____
_____

Power I needed: _____
_____

Queen I called on: _____

Perceptions: _____
_____
_____
_____
_____
_____
_____
_____

Feelings: _____
_____
_____
_____
_____
_____

Message/Images/symbols received: _____

_____

_____

_____

_____

_____

_____

To me this means: _____

_____

_____

_____

_____

_____

_____

_____

End result: _____

_____

_____

_____

_____

_____

_____

Appendix

COMMON TAROT DECKS

P resented here is a list of commonly used Tarot decks with a guide to correspondences with the Queen Up system.

This list is by no means representative of the thousands of decks on the market. If your favorite deck is not listed here, trust your intuition to lead you to interpret the correspondences between the suits. Remember the elemental correspondences in this system and apply that to the suits in your deck. For example, Pentacles correspond to the Earth element and represent health, wealth, and stability. Gems, Coins, Stones, Diamonds, and so on will correspond with this suit. Likewise, the Queen of Swords is the Warrior Queen, associated with Fire. Therefore, a deck with a Queen of Spears would correspond. The Queen of Cups is the loving, nurturing mother, and her element is Water. In other decks she may be called the Queen of Hearts or the Queen of Chalices. The Queen of Wands represents Air and the intellect and creativity, and in other decks she is called the Queen of Rods or Clubs.

Although the general outline below details which specific decks align with one view or another, remember that the most important source of guidance on this path is your intuition. What feels right for you? Simply remember that you are working with archetypal elemental energies and different cultures and schools of thought will assign different names to these energies. Trust your intuition to bring you into contact with the deck with which you have the greatest affinity and with the correspondence that fits with your personal paradigm.

Rider-Waite (also called Waite-Smith) Deck

A. E. Waite and Pamela Colman-Smith, U.S. Games Systems, Inc.

The Queens bear the same names as the Queens in this system; however, interpretations based on some teachings of the Tarot will attribute Wands to the element of Fire (Swords in the Queen Up System) and vice versa.

Thoth Tarot Deck

Aleister Crowley and Frieda Harris, U.S. Games Systems, Inc., originally published by Ordo Templi Orientis in 1969

This deck shows a similar reversal between the Queens of Wands and Swords as described above. In this deck the Queen of Disks corresponds to the Inner Queen of Pentacles in the Queen Up system.

Deviant Moon Tarot

Patrick Valenza, U.S. Games Systems, Inc., 2008

The Queens in this deck follow the suits of Wands, Swords, Cups, and Pentacles. The Queens in this system translate well to the elemental/archetypal correspondences in the Queen Up system.

Wildwood Tarot

Mark Ryan, Sterling Ethos, 2011

This deck offers different names for the Queens. The Queen of Arrows would correspond to the Inner Queen of Wands; the Queen of Bows, to the Inner Queen of Swords. The Queen of Vessels corresponds to the Inner Queen of Cups, and the Queen of Stones to the Inner Queen of Pentacles.

Morgan-Greer

Bill Greer, Lloyd Morgan, U.S. Games Systems, Inc., 1979

There are slight variations. The Queen of Rods would correspond to the Inner Queen of Wands. Otherwise, Swords, Cups, and Pentacles would correspond to Queens of the same name in this system.

Russian Tarot of St. Petersburg

Yury Shakov, Cynthia Giles, U.S. Games Systems, Inc., 1992

The Inner Queen of Wands corresponds to the Queen of Clubs. The Inner Queen of Pentacles corresponds to the Queen of Coins. Swords and Cups correspond to the Queen of the same name in this system.

Gaian Tarot

Joanna Powell Colbert, Schiffer Publishing Ltd., 2016

Queens are called "Guardians" of Air, Fire, Water, and Earth in this system. Thus the Guardian of Air would be the Inner Queen of Wands. The Guardian of Fire corresponds to the Inner Queen of Swords. The Guardian of Water is the Inner Queen of Cups, and the Guardian of Earth is the Inner Queen of Pentacles.

Robin Wood Deck

D. J. Conway, Llewellyn Publication, Cards Edition, 2002

This deck matches the Queen Up system both in names of the Queens (Queen of Wands, Swords, Cups and Pentacles) but also in their elemental association.

Golden Tarot Deck

Kat Black, U.S. Games Systems, Inc., 2004

Substitute the Queen of Coins in this deck for the Queen of Pentacles in the Queen Up system. The remaining three Queens are of the same name.

Mary-El Tarot

Marie White, Schiffer Publishing Ltd., 2012

Substitute the Queen of Disks in this deck for the Queen of Pentacles in the Queen Up system.

Enchanted Tarot Deck

Amy Zerner and Monte Farber, Connections, 2009

Substitute the Queen of Hearts in this deck for the Queen of Cups in the Queen Up system.

Lo Scarabeo Tarot

Mark McElroy and Anna Lazzarini, Lo Scarabeo, 2007

Substitute the Queen of Coins in this deck for the Inner Queen of Pentacles in the Queen Up system.

Grand Etteilla Tarot

Grimaud, 1969

This deck contains suits with different names. The Queen of Rods in this deck corresponds to the Inner Queen of Wands in the Queen Up system. Substitute the Queen of Ducats for the Queen of Pentacles.

Minchiate Tarot

Lo Scarabeo, 2011

This deck is a precursor of modern Tarot and contains a different structure than decks following the modern Rider-Waite system. This deck contains elemental cards for Air, Fire, Water, and Earth, as well as Queens of Staves (Wands), Swords, Cups, and Coins (Pentacles). You may substitute the Element cards for their corresponding Inner Queen (Air = Wands, Fire = Swords, Water = Cups, Earth = Pentacles).

Sola Busca

Lo Scarabeo, 2000

There is a similar structure, but substitute the Queen of Chalices for the Inner Queen of Cups in the Queen Up system.

African American Tarot

Jamal R., Lo Scarabeo, 2007

As in the deck above, the Queen of Chalices in this deck corresponds to the Inner Queen of Cups.

Afro-Brazilian Tarot

Giuseppe Palumbo, Lo Scarabeo, 2006

Substitute the Queen of Chalices for the Inner Queen of Cups.

Tarot of the Orishas

Durkon, Zolrak, Llewellyn, 2013

There are no court cards, but you can use the element cards for Air, Fire, Water, and Earth, as well as the Mermaids/Undines, Fairies and Sylphs, Salamanders, and Elves and Gnomes. Correspondences are:

- Air/Fairies/Sylphs: Inner Queen of Wands
- Fire/Salamanders: Inner Queen of Swords
- Water/Mermaids/Undines: Inner Queen of Cups
- Earth/Elves/Gnomes: Inner Queen of Pentacles

Celtic Tarot

Courtney Davis and Helena Paterson, Thorsons, 1990

Substitute the Queen of Coins for the Inner Queen of Pentacles.

Queen Up with Playing Cards

A standard Bicycle Deck can be used with the Queen Up system as well. The Queen of Clubs corresponds to the Inner Queen of Wands, the Queen of Spades corresponds to the Inner Queen of Swords, the Queen of Hearts to the Inner Queen of Cups, and the Queen of Diamonds to the Inner Queen of Pentacles.

Make Your Own Inner Queen Cards

The Queens that illustrate this book were specifically designed as empowerment tools for the Queen Up system. You may also feel inspired to create your own cards based on the Queen Up correspondences. Use index cards or card stock cut to fit a size of your choosing. The key is portability, so make sure you choose a size that fits comfortably in your hands.

Sit quietly and ask your Higher Self/Spirit Guides for assistance in selecting images or symbols that will trigger your intuition. Trust that your guides are stepping up to the plate to help you through this process.

Review the correspondences below and for each, make a list of colors, symbols, images, and feelings that connect to the concepts. Ask yourself, "What images or scenes make me think of these words?" As these images come to your awareness, jot them down.

Correspondences

Queen of Wands—Air/Intellect—communication, creativity, ideals

Queen of Swords—Fire/Passion—courage, willpower, motivation

Queen of Cups—Water/Emotion—intuition, love, relationships, healing

Queen of Pentacles—Earth/Abundance—wealth, security, physical resources, health

Once you have your list, you may draw your own symbols, or cut out images from magazines, or draw, paint, or create your own representations of each Queen. Use one card to represent each Queen. Remember to draw on color associations as well as images. Have fun with this process!

Meditation Resources

The meditations in this book can be downloaded as audible files. This will allow you to completely relax into your meditation practice without having to break your focus by reading each step. Over time, with repetition, the meditations will become second nature to you, but having them on hand to listen to can enhance your practice. Inner Queen MP3 Meditations are available at the following link: http://intuitiveangela.com/meditationsignup/.

Acknowledgments

I am extremely thankful to my editor Kathryn Sky-Peck and the Conari Press team for bringing this concept into manifestation. Thank you also to Theresa Smolen, who developed the catchphrase "Queen Up!" Thank you to Heather Woodward, for inspiring me to work with archetypes, and to my soul sister Julie MacDonald for encouraging me to take the journey further. Thank you to Sarah Gold for your expertise, and to Julie Ann Price, Kerry Endres, Jane Baldauf, Caryn Zeh, and Ann Voorhees Baker for your creative support. Thank you Jeanine Corina Hughes, who said, "You need to make an Inner Queen planner." Linda Lowen, thank you for your guidance and encouragement to think big. Before *Queen Up* was a book, it was a way. Patricia Gardner and Dayna Winters, thank you for showing me how to align with the elements. Thank you also to my family, to my uncle Dominic Angerame for the gift of my first Tarot deck, and to Jim Hesch for your love, support, and understanding. Thank you Divine Spirit, for your guidance and strength.

Special thanks to Shaheen Miro, artist, Tarot reader, and psychic intuitive, who put his special talent to work to create the beautiful cards that are the backbone of the Queen Up system.

My immense thanks to you as well, reader, for your courage and trust. It is you who will carry the energy of empowerment from these pages into reality, making the world a better place.

Photo by Deborah Neary

About the Author

Angela Kaufman has been a lifelong seeker of spiritual connection. As a teen, she began to explore Wicca, Tarot, and metaphysics as well as mythology, psychology, and art.

Blending the mystical and the practical, it is Angela's mission to help others connect with the world of Spirit for healing, growth, and understanding. Her current work as an intuitive relationship and empowerment coach is based on training as a clinical social worker, certified intuitive consultant, psychic medium and her personal journey. She conducts small group workshops to lead other women on the path to empowerment using the Queen Up! system.

Angela has coauthored several books including *Wicca, What's the Real Deal? Breaking Through the Misconceptions* (Schiffer 2011), *Sacred Objects, Sacred Space: Everyday Tools for the Modern Day Witch* (Schiffer 2012), and *The Esoteric Dream Book: Mastering the Magickal Symbolism of the Subconscious Mind* (Schiffer 2013) with Patricia Gardner and Dayna Winters. She also enjoys writing fiction and short stories and creating spiritually inspired art.

Angela invites you to join empowered seekers like yourself in the Royal Court Inner Queen community on Facebook at *www.facebook .com/groups/951352234902895/*

To Our Readers

Conari Press, an imprint of Red Wheel/Weiser, publishes books on topics ranging from spirituality, personal growth, and relationships to women's issues, parenting, and social issues. Our mission is to publish quality books that will make a difference in people's lives—how we feel about ourselves and how we relate to one another. We value integrity, compassion, and receptivity, both in the books we publish and in the way we do business.

Our readers are our most important resource, and we appreciate your input, suggestions, and ideas about what you would like to see published. Visit our website at *www.redwheelweiser.com* to learn about our upcoming books and free downloads, and be sure to go to *www.redwheelweiser.com/newsletter* to sign up for newsletters and exclusive offers. You can also contact us at *info@rwwbooks.com*.

Conari Press
an imprint of Red Wheel/Weiser, LLC
65 Parker Street, Suite 7
Newburyport, MA 01950
www.redwheelweiser.com